# THE
# REVENUE GROWTH HABIT

# THE
# REVENUE GROWTH HABIT

## THE SIMPLE ART OF GROWING YOUR BUSINESS BY 15% IN 15 MINUTES A DAY

### ALEX GOLDFAYN

WILEY

Published by John Wiley & Sons, Inc., Hoboken, New Jersey.
Published simultaneously in Canada.

For general information about our other products and services, please contact our Customer Care Department within the United States at (800) 762-2974, outside the United States at (317) 572-3993 or fax (317) 572-4002.

Wiley publishes in a variety of print and electronic formats and by print-on-demand. Some material included with standard print versions of this book may not be included in e-books or in print-on-demand. If this book refers to media such as a CD or DVD that is not included in the version you purchased, you may download this material at http://booksupport.wiley.com. For more information about Wiley products, visit www.wiley.com.

*Library of Congress Cataloging-in-Publication Data:*

Goldfayn, Alex L.
  The revenue growth habit : the simple art of growing your business by 15% in 15 minutes a day / Alex Goldfayn.
     pages cm
  Includes index.
  ISBN 978-1-119-08406-8 (cloth); ISBN 978-1-119-08404-4 (ebk);
ISBN 978-1-119-08405-1 (ebk)
  1.  Strategic planning.  2.  Revenue management.  I.  Title.
  HD30.28.G645 2015
  658.15'54–dc23

                                                            2015013431

Printed in the United States of America

10 9 8 7 6 5 4 3 2 1

# Contents

*Acknowledgments*                                                                    *ix*

*Introduction    You Deserve More Revenue*                                            *xi*

*Download Revenue Growth Forms and Templates*                                        *xiii*

**PART ONE**     **The Simple Revenue Growth Process**

**Chapter 1**    Revenue Growth Is Fast, Simple, and Free                              3

**Chapter 2**    Here's What Your Growth Plan Will Look Like by the
                 End of This Book                                                     11

**Chapter 3**    Why Do You Work?                                                     15

**PART TWO**     **The Growth Mindset—Change Your Thinking,
                 Grow Your Business**

**Chapter 4**    It's Impossible to Outmarket Your Mindset                            21

**Chapter 5**    "But I'm Already Really Busy!"                                        27

**Chapter 6**    The Difference between Knowing and Doing                             31

**Chapter 7**    The Mind-Numbingly Simple Definition of Marketing                    37

**Chapter 8**    The Only Meaningful Measure of Marketing                             41

**Chapter 9**    It Really Is This Simple!                                            45

**Chapter 10** Your Products and Services Are Much Better Than Your Marketing 49

**Chapter 11** "We Don't Like to Brag" 61

**Chapter 12** Frequently Raised Resistance (FRR) 65

**Chapter 13** Your Customers Speak More Positively about You than You Speak about Yourself 71

**Chapter 14** Marinating in Positivity: The Magic of Proactive Customer Conversations 75

**PART THREE** **22 Fast, Simple Techniques for Revenue Growth**

**Chapter 15** What These 22 Revenue Growth Techniques Have in Common 81

**Chapter 16** Choreographing Your Revenue Growth Dance 87

**Chapter 17** Growth Technique #1: The Art and Science of Getting the Testimonial 89

**Chapter 18** Lessons from a Sample Customer Interview 97

**Chapter 19** Growth Technique #2: Don't Be a Tree Falling in the Forest—Communicate Testimonials 109

**Chapter 20** Growth Technique #3: Create Short, Powerful Case Studies 117

**Chapter 21** Growth Technique #4: Communicate Case Studies to People Who Can Buy from You 121

**Chapter 22** Growth Technique #5: The Million-Dollar Question— This One Technique Can Grow Your Business by 10% Immediately 125

**Chapter 23** Growth Technique #6: How to Get Referrals 133

**Chapter 24** Growth Technique #7: The Power of Owner Calls 139

**Chapter 25**   Growth Technique #8: The Seven-Figure
Follow-Up Process                                                141

**Chapter 26**   Growth Technique #9: The Magic of the
Handwritten Note                                                 145

**Chapter 27**   Growth Technique #10: Communicate with Your
High-Potential Small Customers (HPSCs)                           149

**Chapter 28**   Growth Technique #11: Create Your Own Social
Media—Relentlessly Grow Your Lists                              155

**Chapter 29**   Growth Technique #12: Categorizing for Revenue
Growth—How to Organize Your Lists                               161

**Chapter 30**   Growth Technique #13: Send a Wildly Valuable
Newsletter to Your List                                          165

**Chapter 31**   Growth Technique #14: Growth by White Papers    171

**Chapter 32**   Growth Technique #15: Turning Trade Shows
into Revenue                                                     173

**Chapter 33**   Growth Technique #16: Host an Unforgettable Event
for Customers and Prospects                                      175

**Chapter 34**   Growth Technique #17: Speak(er) the Truth—
You're the Expert                                                179

**Chapter 35**   Growth Technique #18: Conduct Webinars That Bring
New Business                                                     183

**Chapter 36**   Growth Technique #19: How to Grow Your Business
with Videos                                                      185

**Chapter 37**   Growth Technique #20: Public Relationships—How to
Leverage the Media for Revenue Growth                           191

**Chapter 38**   Growth Technique #21: Price Increases Are a
Growth Technique!                                                195

**Chapter 39**   Growth Technique #22: The Single Most Important
Website Edit for Revenue Growth                                      199

**Chapter 40**   Growth Techniques by Job Title                      203

**PART FOUR**   **Executing the Plan**

**Chapter 41**   Action Is Everything                                209

**Chapter 42**   How Perfection and Procrastination Kill Revenue     211

**Chapter 43**   Why 15 Minutes? Because It's Enough to Grow Your
Business Dramatically                                                215

**Chapter 44**   Introducing the 15-Minute Marketing® Planner        217

**Chapter 45**   What Sets My Most Successful Clients Apart
(Accountability)                                                     223

**Chapter 46**   Grow Forth and Execute                              227

*Appendix*   *Workbook for Launching the Revenue Growth Habit*        *229*

*Index*                                                               *235*

# Acknowledgments

My gratitude to Richard Narramore, my terrific editor at John Wiley & Sons, who fought for this book when it was in proposal form. Thanks to Matt Holt for buying into Richard's obviously exceptional reasoning. I also appreciate the work of Wendy Keller, Tiffany Colon, Linda Indig, and Cape Cod Compositors.

I've been blessed in my career to experience and learn from the great depths of professional struggle, which have allowed me to properly appreciate the hard-earned heights this work has brought my family to. I have suffered for my art, and so, too, has my bride, who I have been with for more than half my life. Throughout this great roller coaster, on many difficult days, weeks, months, and years, Lisa's belief and support have never wavered. There is no "this" without you.

I know who I work for.

I work for my son, Noah, who teaches me through his boundless optimism and joy, and my daughter, Bella, whose thoughtful kindness sometimes stops me in my tracks.

I work for my dad, Leon, who dragged his family, me included, out of the former Soviet Union in the 1970s when there was no Internet. He didn't know English, had no money, and had no family here. His great courage then inspires me now.

I work for my mom, Jane, who told me to write early and often (well, that and to be a doctor; sorry about that one, Mom). But you were right about the writing! My mom doesn't know how to stop. That trait has helped me greatly.

I work for my amazing grandmother, Bella, who I have been fortunate to have into my middle age. People are drawn to her as if she's a magnet. She teaches me with her empathy and great intelligence.

And I work for my clients, all the entrepreneurs, and business owners whose risks often far outweigh their rewards. It's frequently thankless work—not glamorous as it is perceived. Your simple recipe to revenue growth is within these pages.

I work for you. I am grateful to you.

# Introduction
# You Deserve More Revenue

You deserve more revenue.

Your products or services provide great value for your customers.

If you asked them, your customers would tell you that you make their lives easier. Working with you helps save your customers countless hours. You make your customers look good to *their* customers and also to their boss, if they have one. They consider you a partner, not a supplier or provider. They trust you. They value you. *You help them.*

As such, they deserve to buy more from you. (And they actually would buy more, if given the opportunity to know about your other products, lines, options, and services. More on this throughout the book.) Your existing customers deserve to benefit more from your value. And you deserve the top-line income that results from that.

Further, your prospects, the people who have not yet bought from you, deserve to benefit from your value as well. Why would you want to keep your tremendous value from them?

When you call on your customers and prospects, you're not bothering them, you're not imposing, you're not wasting their time, and you're not trying to get their business. *You're helping them.* And if we're in this world to help people, you owe your customers and prospects the opportunity to enjoy and benefit from your value. They deserve it. And you deserve the revenue that results.

You know who else deserves that you generate more revenue?

*Your family.* They deserve to enjoy the benefits of your hard work. Yes, they also deserve the things that money can buy—the nice home, the vacations, and the good schools (after all, most of us work to help take care of our families).

*Your colleagues and your staff,* who deserve to work for a thriving organization.

*Your suppliers,* who stand by you even when times are tough.

And, of course, you. *You* deserve more revenue. You work too hard, take too much risk, and provide too much value to your customers to not be making more money.

*I'm doing fine,* you say?

I think you can be doing better. You have low-hanging revenue fruit, and I'm going to help you pick it.

*It's not that simple,* you think?

Revenue growth is quite simple: It's fast, it's easy, and it requires no financial investment. One of the dumbest widely accepted so-called truths in business is that it takes money to make money. People also like to say that revenue growth is a complicated pursuit requiring a lot of time. These beliefs are simply untrue. In this book, I will teach you how to grow your organization by 15% or more in 15 minutes or less a day without spending a penny of your money. To grow your revenue, we'll need just a bit of your personal effort every day. Some days it'll be 60 seconds, other days five minutes, but never more than 15 minutes a day.

You help your customers in great ways, and they deserve to buy more from you.

And you deserve to enjoy the revenue that results and all the experiences, improvements, and peace of mind that it can buy for you and your family.

# Download Revenue Growth Forms and Templates

You can download clean copies of the templates and forms throughout this book, including the 15-Minute Marketing® Planner, at www.RevenueGrowthHabit.com.

    If you're a business owner, visit RevenueGrowthForum.com to discuss the concepts in this book with your peers and directly with me. It's a private growth community for business owners focused on quickly and dramatically increasing sales. I'll answer your questions personally there.

There is no cost.

# PART
## ONE

# The Simple Revenue Growth Process

# 1 | Revenue Growth Is Fast, Simple, and Free

Today, I run a seven-figure revenue-growth consulting practice by myself, out of my home. It's a very successful business, and there are few sole proprietorships with zero employees at this level.

But not that long ago, I would go to bed praying that I could feed my family, and when it comes to prayers, I don't really know what I'm doing. I had just changed business models, and I was going through the process of learning how to consult. There were months when we were literally out of money. It was a painful, anxious, frightening time, seared into my brain. Frankly, it was my greatest fear coming true. I promised myself that if I got things turned around, I would never be in that position again.

And then I started developing and applying my Revenue Growth Habit—the mindset changes and quick behaviors that make up this book. The techniques laid out in these pages were designed for my clients. But, they also moved my business from the struggle to serious success.

The Revenue Growth Habit turned my business around quickly, and transformed it into the thriving consultancy I run today. I don't think about running out of money anymore, because I know that when a need for additional revenue arises, I can simply dial up the techniques in this book. They are like a rheostat, to be adjusted upwards and downwards, as needed.

These approaches have also grown the companies of dozens of clients by 10% to 20% in their first year with me. One client told me recently that his net profit is up by 100% as a result of our work together. Additionally, thousands of people in the audiences I speak to have successfully developed their own Revenue Growth Habit using just some of the techniques in this book.

I am sharing this with you not to be boastful. Rather, I want you to know that these are not just ideas. They are not merely concepts on the page, theories spoken from the stage. The mindset and behaviors I will teach you in this book have significantly grown thousands of businesses. Over the years, around the world, the Revenue Growth Habit has generated hundreds of millions of dollars of new revenue.

The best part? Growing your sales with my approaches is simple, free, and eminently doable. You can increase your revenue by 15% or more in 15 minutes a day, just like the subtitle of this book says, and the only investment that's required is a bit of your effort. I will tell you what to do. If you can give me 15 minutes a day, maximum, I will teach you how to dramatically grow your company.

## Who This Book Is For

Although my direct clients are almost always owners of closely held companies worth between $5 million and $2 billion, *The Revenue Growth Habit* is for anyone who's interested in increasing sales: owners, CEOs, presidents, vice presidents, general managers, salespeople, marketers, and customer service professionals. Who can benefit from this book? Anyone who has a customer-facing job. Does your company have delivery drivers? They see customers, therefore, they can implement one or two of the techniques in this book to help grow your company. If you're an owner, share these principles with your teams. If you interact with customers in any capacity whatsoever—in person, on the phone, or even only by email—you will find many powerful approaches here to significantly grow your company's sales.

## Your Today: Busy and Reactive to Customer Problems

I know you, and I understand you.

You're a business owner, executive, manager, or frontline staff member in sales, or customer service, or marketing.

You're extremely busy. You spend your days dealing with customers' concerns and complaints.

*"My order is late! Where is it?!"*

*"You screwed it up. Get it right!"*

*"Are you serious?! That price is way too high!"*

Customers never call when they're happy. Nobody ever calls to say, *"Hey, great job, that was really well done, we really appreciate what you did there."* We only hear from people when something is wrong. They bring us their fires, place them upon our desks, and we must put them out immediately lest our eyebrows get singed. As soon as that fire is out, what happens? The next one comes along. *"Here's MY fire, don't get burned!"*

And so, you spend your days reacting to one such urgent concern after another. If you're lucky you squeeze in lunch at your desk or in your car, but it's probably overcooked by the day's fires.

Your days are reactive, but revenue growth is proactive work.

*We must make time for it.*

The good news: Revenue growth does not require hours daily. Or even an hour.

You can grow your organization by 15% or more in 15 minutes or less a day.

Do you have 15 minutes?

I do. My clients, the owners of 7-, 8-, 9-, and 10-figure firms do.

Do you?

## Your Tomorrow: Proactively Growing Your Sales in 15 Minutes or Less Daily

If you've made it to this section, I'm assuming you've decided you have 90 seconds, or 3 minutes, but no more than 15 minutes a day to commit to growing your organization.

We'll use this time for the proactive work of communicating your company's value to people who can buy it. (That's my definition of marketing, by the way. Simple, right? More on this definition in Chapter 7.)

Each day, I'd like you to take one quick, proactive action that tells somebody something about how they'll be improved after they buy from you.

You can select any of the 22 actions listed in Part Three of this book.

Every one of these techniques is fast, because revenue growth does not require a lot of time.

These techniques are free, because revenue growth costs no money.

They're simple, because the simplest solution is almost always the right one, and the tools I'm going to arm you with are incredibly easy to execute.

These approaches require your personal effort, because personal communication is going the way of the BlackBerry. Personal communication helps you stand out.

These techniques are communications actions. They demand that you communicate your value to somebody who can buy it from you. For example: I will teach you how to request and collect testimonials. But more importantly, you will learn how to *communicate* these testimonials to grow your business. I will teach you how to write a powerful case study, but more importantly, I'll arm you with the best ways to *communicate* that case study. I'll also teach you how your customer service people, who take incoming calls all day, can inform your current customers about what else they can buy from you.

My approaches revolve around letting your customers tell your story. There is nothing you can say about your products and services that is more effective than what your paying customers say. So, in many of these revenue growth techniques, we quote your customers. We tell their stories, because as a part of this approach, they will have given us permission to do so. We will make clear how they have been improved since they've worked with you. And we will allow them to compare you to your competition. When we're done, the prospect will be thinking, "I want that too! How can I get that kind of value?"

We will not use social media as a tool because social media does not grow revenue. Listen to me carefully on this, especially if you are in a business-to-business market: You can be on social media if you'd like to be, but understand that it will not grow your business. Any revenue you generate because of your activities on Facebook, Twitter, and probably even LinkedIn is an accident. Social media is not where decision makers go to decide about making major—or even minor—business investments. Where *do* they go? To their peers. To their colleagues. To their industry trade shows and publications. *This* is the kind of communication we will place before these decision makers. We will bring the emotional endorsements of your customers—their peers—to them directly.

I don't care which technique you use.

I don't care what time of day you take your action.

I only care that every day you tell an existing customer about what else she can buy from you, and how she'll improve as a result. Or maybe you will tell a prospect about the great ways you can help him. You can tell one person a day. Or 1,000 by email.

There's no wrong way.

If only you *do* some of this work, if you execute, you can't screw this up.

## It All Begins with Your Mindset

In Part Two, we'll talk about how to shift your mindset so you can grow revenue quickly.

It is impossible to outmarket and outsell your mindset. You must believe the right things about your business. That is, you must focus on how your customers are improved by what you sell rather than the products and services you sell. The latter is a commodity—people can buy your products and services from anyone. The former, however, is singular: Your value, your relationships, your trusted reputation—your customers can only obtain these from you. Your competition can't touch this. It's what sets you apart from everybody else. Talk about your products and services, and you're just like everybody else: boring, unemotional, commoditized. Talk about your value (which is exactly what your customers talk about when, as a part of nearly every consulting project I do, I ask them what they like best about working with you) and you'll stand miles apart from the crowd.

We can only communicate what we believe about ourselves. If we believe we sell products and services, that's what we'll talk about. If we believe we improve lives and companies—which is precisely what we do— we'll talk about that. So, before we can grow revenue, before we can develop this habit that will increase our top line, we must shift our thinking from what we sell and do to how our customers are improved by working with us.

Your staff and your colleagues are probably somewhat beaten down. Customers only call when they're unhappy or when there's a problem. As such, your colleagues and staff members probably spend their days dealing predominantly with negative feedback. But the truth is, if you only asked your customers, they'd tell you that they're very happy doing business with you. That's why they've been with you for years or decades. They have a lot of options, competition calls on them all the time, yet they stay with you. I will teach you how to draw out the positive thoughts and feelings of your customers. I will teach you how to use them internally to align your staff's perception of your work with that of your customers. As a client recently told me, perhaps more than anything else, this is a positive endeavor.

## Ready?

This work is simple, fast, and free. You can do everything laid out in this book yourself. You can implement the Revenue Growth Habit at your own firm, using this book as a guide. (And if you want to add outside expertise and accountability into your mix, I'm happy to create new revenue for you, with you.)

In revenue growth, ironically, quantity trumps quality. The more customers and prospects hear from you, the more they will buy. It doesn't have to be amazing material, only helpful material. Helpful is more than good enough. Helpful is a rare commodity. The important thing is that people hear from you a lot, not perfectly.

Finally, don't wait to communicate until it's perfect, because it will never be. We must move our communication into the world when it's good enough, not when it's perfect. Perfection slows us down, makes us over-think, and ultimately, procrastinate. Quick, systematic, repetitive communication is what's required to grow small and mid-sized businesses.

Commit to start, and the very day you're done with this book, take one action from Part Three in 15 minutes or 90 seconds. If you are so inclined, feel free to take one action today. Action begets more action. Leverage physics. Develop your Revenue Growth Habit.

Ready?

Let's go!

**Chapter Summary**

- This book is for owners, presidents, and leaders of small and mid-sized companies. It's also for your salespeople, customer service people, and all other customer-facing staff.
- You likely spend your days reacting to customer problems today, addressing one urgent concern after the next.
- Revenue growth is proactive work. We must make time for it.

# 2 | Here's What Your Growth Plan Will Look Like by the End of This Book

The Revenue Growth Habit will grow your business because when you develop it, customers and prospects will hear from you far more than they're currently hearing from you.

When your Revenue Growth Habit is in full effect, you will have two parallel tracks of communications occurring simultaneously:

### The One-on-One Communications Track

These communications will be made by your salespeople, customer service people, and executives to customers and prospects. These activities are done in person, on the phone, by email, by snail mail, and any other way you can think of to communicate your value to people who can buy it.

### The Company-to-Many Communications Track

This track of communications is what business schools call direct marketing. These activities begin with a good list of your customers

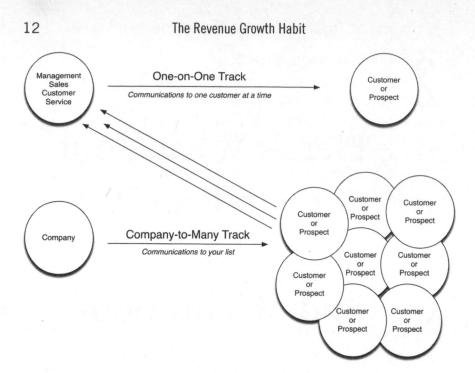

**Figure 2.1   The Revenue Growth Habit Is Made Up of Two Parallel Tracks of Communication**

and prospects and a consistent newsletter that demonstrates your amazing value to customers and prospects. A list and a high-value news-letter make for an excellent start to this track. Then we can add in other elements like sending testimonials and case studies, distributing a white paper, or holding webinars and live meetings. Ideally, this process is managed by a marketing quarterback who oversees its execution.

Figure 2.1 shows what these two tracks look like in action.

The customer or prospect receiving your one-on-one communications on the top track is also on the list of customers and prospects on the bottom track. Therefore, once you start implementing your revenue growth habit, your customers and prospects will be hearing from you exponentially more than they hear from you now.

The diagonal arrow in Figure 2.1 is what I call "hand-raising," wherein people on your list, who are receiving your company-to-many marketing raise their hands and tell your salespeople, "I'm interested, tell me more."

Here are some keys to this approach:

### You're Not Selling, You're Marketing

That is, in these communications, you're not pitching, pushing, selling, or closing. Rather, you're telling people how they will be improved when they buy (or buy more) from you. Also, and this is very important: in these two tracks of communications, you're *helping* people. You're providing value. Your goal is to make the recipients of these communications say, "If they can help me this much for free in these newsletters, imagine what they can do for me if I work with them."

### It's All About One Quick Activity a Day

The key to this simple plan is that you *and your colleagues* execute one communications activity a day in 90 seconds or 15 minutes. This is the proactive work that business growth requires. One action, and you've marketed for the day. Then, you simply continue on with the rest of your regular, reactive day. Meanwhile, the same people will be hearing from your firm on the company-to-many track.

### Let Your Customers Say It

If *you* tell me you're wonderful and amazing, I'll figure you're just selling to me. If your paying customers tell me you're great, I can't argue with it. There's no defense against happy customers communicating what they're pleased about. It's the truth. Therefore, we must use testimonials and case studies to tell our story.

### Consistency Is Key

You must be reliable. It's better to have no newsletter at all than have a monthly newsletter that comes five times per year. The latter will hurt you more than the former: it costs you the hard-earned trust of your market.

As you can see, this approach forces you to systematically, quickly, and consistently communicate with people who can buy from you. If you have

10 people in sales and customer service, you'll execute a minimum of 10 one-on-one communications a day, or 200 per month, or 2,400 per year. And if only half of your people execute the plan, that's still well over 1,000 communications that are probably not being done today. And I'm not even counting the list-based communication on the company-to-many track.

This is why I say that with the Revenue Growth Habit, your business has no choice but to grow.

---

**Chapter Summary**

- Your revenue growth habit will consist of two parallel tracks of communication—one-on-one, and company-to-many.
- The one-on-one track includes private communications to one customer or prospect at a time.
- The company-to-many track is based upon your list of customers and prospects and features communications that go to the entire list, like your newsletter.
- One communication activity a day, along either track, is enough to grow your business significantly.

# 3 | Why Do You Work?

For leaders of small and mid-size companies, revenue growth requires some personal growth. The two are closely interconnected.

One of the most important first steps is to identify *why we work, who we work for,* and to be *consciously aware of it while we work.*

Let me tell you the story of my *raison d'être* and perhaps it will help you identify (or recall or create) yours.

I was born in the Ukraine, when it was a part of the Soviet Union. We lived in the western part of the country, on the border of Poland in a city called L'vov.

My family lived in a 400-square-foot government-issued apartment, as all apartments in Ukraine were back then. Six of us lived inside that dark, drab space: my mom and dad, my grandmother and grandfather, and my great-grandmother. There were two rooms. My grandparents slept on a pullout couch in the living room, every night.

In the late 1970s, my dad decided, as a 25-year-old, that he wanted to move to America. He had heard wonderful things about the country, but back then, the United States was the enemy. It's not like he could study English in Ukraine; people were afraid to teach it. And in my family, he was the only person who wanted to leave. My grandparents, who were already retired, didn't want to leave the only country they had ever known. My mom was afraid, because she had watched movies like *The Godfather*, and thought perhaps everyone was like that here. Further, the world was a whole lot bigger back then. There was no Internet to research cities you might choose to make your home. There were no message boards, experience sharing, or online ads.

But, with $23 in cash, my dad dragged the family out and to the United States. I was two years old.

Recently, I went back to L'vov with my parents to see that tiny apartment. The people who live in the apartment now were expecting us, they had been told we were coming. They let us in. There are eight people living there now. It felt claustrophobic. I tried imagining myself living there now as an adult. I couldn't.

The mood in Ukraine is not prosperous.

The environment is not entrepreneurial.

The average citizen makes a few hundred dollars per month, mostly from government assistance.

That was a defining trip in my life.

Here's what it crystallized.

I work for my dad.

I take the risks that I take for my family, my dad and my mom, who brought me from that place to the greatest country in the world so that I could have a better life.

I struggled in business for years, because in the United States, I *get* to struggle in order to succeed.

And because of that struggle and the great learning and development that came of it, I now run a highly successful seven-figure practice helping my clients grow their top lines quickly and dramatically. Think I would be doing this if my dad didn't put the family on his back and bring us here?

Because I grew up here, and went to university here, I got to meet my wonderful wife here. (Her background is an only-in-America Polish-Italian-English-Swedish one.) I work for her. There were days—months, even—where she believed in me more than I believed in myself. She deserves my success more than anyone. She deserves my revenue growth.

And because I live in the United States, I am the incredibly proud father of young twins, a son and a daughter, who bring me great joy and pleasure every moment of every day. I work for them. I fight for them. I owe them.

You know who else I work for? That family who lives in that Ukrainian apartment today. They don't get to be entrepreneurs and risk-takers. They don't get to enjoy everything I was lucky enough to enjoy growing up.

And here, perhaps, is the greatest lesson you can take away from my story: In America, your level of success, and, indeed, your revenue, is determined only by your effort and your perseverance.

*So, who do you work for?*

It's important to get clear on this.

It's important because it helps you wake up happy and jump out of bed with energy and happiness, even if you have a day full of activities you'd rather not tackle.

When you're clear on why you work, you don't hesitate to pick up the phone.

You don't feel like you're imposing on your prospect's time.

You don't procrastinate.

You do your work boldly and decisively. Because you know who you're doing it for.

Who do you work for? Who do you take your risks for?

Who do you struggle for?

Think about your story, your journey, which brought you to this day.

Who are the key players? Who deserves your success?

Who do you work for?

---

### Chapter Summary

Being clear on who we work for and why we work makes it easier to be bold and intentional about our communications and revenue growth.

# PART TWO

# The Growth Mindset—Change Your Thinking, Grow Your Business

# 4

# It's Impossible to Outmarket Your Mindset

As we discussed in Part One, how you think about and perceive your business has a massive impact on its growth.

Consider the diagram in Figure 4.1.

Starting at the upper left, your marketing—which is what you communicate about your business to your market—has the single greatest impact on revenue growth. That is, there is nothing you can do in your business—not even sales!—that will grow your company faster, easier, and more impactfully than marketing.

The reason marketing is more impactful than selling is because sales is, by definition, one-on-one. As you read in Chapter 2, marketing can be one-on-one and company-to-many. *Marketing opens what sales closes.* Let me be clear: Under no circumstances am I suggesting that you sell less. No. To grow, we must sell more. Marketing catalyzes increased sales. The more we market, the more sales opportunities arise.

Back to Figure 4.1: If your marketing has the greatest impact on your growth, it is your mindset that impacts your marketing more than anything else. As I've purposefully repeated already, how you think is how you market. If you believe you're helping people and growing companies, you'll

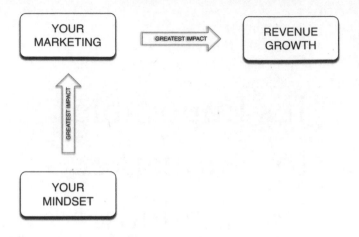

**Figure 4.1    It's Impossible to Outsell or Outmarket Your Mindset**

market that. If you believe you sell parts, and their accompanying (and fascinating) specifications, you'll market those. The former is far more effective, compelling, memorable, and interesting than the latter.

Figure 4.2 offers another way of thinking about this.

Starting at the top: more than anything else, your marketing (1) shapes your market's perceptions (2) of your firm, products, and services. That is,

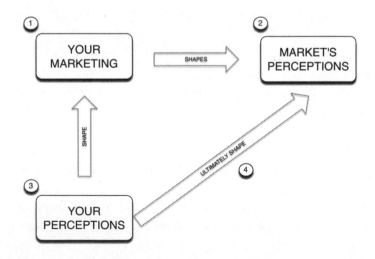

**Figure 4.2    A Transference of Perceptions**

the things you communicate about your company shape how people perceive it. Further, your perceptions of your company, products, and services (3) shape your marketing more than anything else. As such, marketing is nothing more than a transference of perceptions from you onto your market (4).

This is why we begin a revenue growth book with chapters about mindset. Your perceptions of your value shape not only your behavior but the behavior of your market. If you perceive your value to be in your products and services, you will market those items, and your market will perceive you accordingly, as a commodity. Your customers and prospects will price-shop you. They'll beat you up on price. That's because when you're seen as a commodity, all you have to compete on is price. Reputation and past transactions don't come into play, because you're a commodity. Those things don't matter. Because you focus on the things you sell and market them, your customers and prospects perceive you as a seller of those *things*. Almost always, those things are commodities.

Conversely, if you perceive your work based on your value, based on all the different ways you save your customers time; and make them money, and make them look good to their customers, thereby increasing their repeat business and referrals; and make them look good to their bosses, thereby increasing their job security; then you will market this value. You will focus your communications on your relationships. In turn, your customers and prospects will perceive you in exactly this way. And when they're thinking about the ways you improve them, you are singular. When your customers are thinking about your relationship, you have no competition. Price doesn't matter nearly as much. Here, history is important. Trust. Partnership. Friendship. These customers will say they think of you as *family*. Think about that! Who can compete with that?

Nobody.

## Shift Your Thinking

If a focus on products and service commoditizes you, and a focus on value and relationships makes you singular, then you must shift your thinking from what you do and sell to how you improve lives and companies (Figure 4.3).

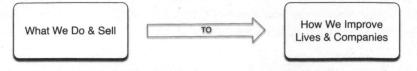

**Figure 4.3    The Critical Revenue Growth Mindset Shift**

When you focus on what you do and sell, your communications focus on the following areas, to the exclusion of the specific ways your customers are improved when they work with you:

- An overemphasis on product and service names and details.
- Including product and service details, processes, and approaches.
- Detailing specifications, speeds, and statistics.
- A focus on you and your stuff.

On the other hand, when you focus on your value these are the kinds of things you communicate:

- How your customers are improved when they work with you.
- Specific details about how your products or work helped your customer make money, save money, save time, become more productive, or become happier.
- Customer testimonials—with names, job titles, and companies.
- Customer case studies, which detail what the customer's problem was when she came to you, what she bought, and how, specifically, it helped her.
- A laser focus on the customer.

When you focus your thinking—and thereby your marketing and selling—on your value and how your customers improve, you behave more confidently. You become bolder. You take more action. You'll sell more. You'll grow your company's revenue. Business will be better. Life will be easier. You will, literally, enjoy life more. And this is not only for owners. The exact same benefits extend to management, staff, and even independent contractors or sales reps you work with. If *they* shift their mindset to your firm's value and away from its products and services, *they* will be bolder, take more action, sell more, and improve their lives.

Focus yourself on how you improve your customers, and you'll grow your business and improve your life.

---

**Chapter Summary**

- Our mindset determines the marketing we put into the world.
- Our perceptions shape how our market perceives us.
- Therefore we must go about trying to shift our thinking from what we make or sell to how it helps our customers and prospects.
- Focus on your value, and the revenue will follow.

# 5

# "But I'm Already Really Busy!"

I know you're busy.

You spend your days managing, selling, responding, helping, processing, answering, detailing, and pouring water on fires so that they don't turn into raging infernos.

You're on the road visiting customers.

You're taking calls from them also, dealing with their problems, frustrations, emergencies, catastrophes, and anger. They scream. You solve their problems. They pat you on the back. They eat the dinners you buy and drink your drinks, and go on your customer appreciation trips. The next day, they're screaming again, and the cycle begins anew.

And we haven't even started talking about what happens inside your company. If the shipping people are behind, you need to run the part to the customer yourself. If your customer service colleagues are swamped on the phones, you're dealing with issues you don't have time for. Conversely, if the salespeople are too busy to deal with this customer, the folks in customer service need to address issues that fall beyond your scope.

I understand what you're dealing with, and what your days are like.

Figure 5.1    **The Reactive Work versus Proactive Work**

And yet, on top of all of this work you already have, I'm asking you to find even more time for this revenue growth work.

That's because, today, like most people, you're busy with *reactive work*—others have a need, and you react to it. You are on the left of the continuum in Figure 5.1. But, as I've already said (if I repeat something, it's important!), revenue growth is *proactive work*. We must move towards the right of this continuum. Not all the way, but just 15 minutes-a-day-worth.

Revenue growth demands that we make time for it.

The Revenue Growth Habit consists of proactive communications to customers and prospects that you're not making today.

If we go through our days drifting from one customer demand to the next, we are not in control of our success. We do not determine our own futures—the universe does. Random issues do. When we're reactive, we are puppies chasing treats, which are the promises of additional business from demanding customers—if only we resolve this current problem.

The following activities are examples of reactive work. These are all completely necessary, even mandatory, behaviors in business. If we didn't do these things, we wouldn't have a business. *But these activities do not grow your business:*

- Answering customer questions.
- Responding to customer complaints.
- Filling/processing orders.
- Creating quotes or estimates.
- Delivering products or services after they've been sold.
- Providing technical support or documentation.
- Every other activity that occurs in response to a customer or a sale.

These activities, on the other hand, are examples of the kind of proactive work that *will* grow your business. We must make time for this kind of work;

it will not occur if we go through our day reactively. The Revenue Growth Habit is about automating this kind of work, one activity a day:

- Informing a customer about what else they can buy from you.
- Asking for a testimonial.
- Communicating a testimonial.
- Asking for a referral.
- Adding contacts to your list.
- Sending a hand-written note to a customer.
- Sending a high-value newsletter to your growing list.

*What do these proactive activities have in common? Four things:*

1. They are almost all communication actions. The recipients of these activities are people who can buy from you.
2. They are all activities we know are important, but they get put on the back-burner by urgent customer issues.
3. They can all be done quickly, in 15 minutes or less.
4. They are all easy to do once you know how to do them. None of these actions are challenging. It's the *doing* that's challenging.

---

### Chapter Summary

- Most people spend their days reacting to urgent customer concerns.
- Revenue growth is proactive work.
- We must make time for revenue growth—just one activity a day, 15 minutes a day.

# 6 | The Difference between Knowing and Doing

You already know what to do.

You're smart. You know this stuff.

I'm not going to teach you very much in this book that you don't already know.

For example, you *know* that you should be asking for more referrals, right?

Similarly, you know that you should have a good list of all your customers and prospects, and you should stay in regular contact with them by *consistently* sending a high-value newsletter.

Right?

The question is, are you doing what you know to do?

Yes, the work is easy.

Yes, you've probably already heard about most of what's in this book.

What's more, you probably deeply understand the importance of doing this work. Your success and your family's well-being are the end result of this effort.

The problem is, if you're like most people, you're probably not doing *enough* of this stuff. Not because you don't want to. But as we discussed in the last chapter, simply because you're extremely busy. One after another, customers make their urgent requests, and you must deliver on them.

## The Distance between Knowing and Doing

So, I hope you agree with me that you are on the left side of the visual depicted in Figure 6.1. And where you want to be is on the right, actually doing what we know we should.

Knowing ———————————→ Doing

**Figure 6.1   The Distance between Knowing and Doing**

What separates them? What's the distance between knowing and doing (and there's really no wrong answer here?

At this point in my speeches and workshops, people suggest some of the following:

- A plan
- Time
- Effort
- Attention
- Procrastination (a personal favorite of mine!)
- Action!

I like all of these, and none of them are incorrect, really. But I think it comes down to another word: *discipline*.

I think discipline is the distance between knowing and doing.
If you know what to do, but you're not doing (enough of) it, you must add discipline into the equation (Figure 6.2).

Which means what, exactly? It's a simple word without a simple definition. *Until now!*

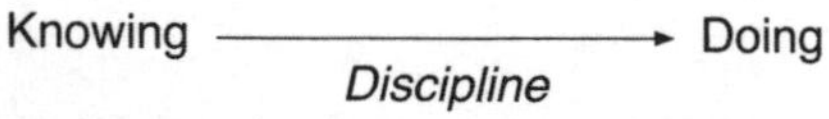

Knowing ———————————→ Doing
*Discipline*

**Figure 6.2   Discipline Gets Us from Knowing to Doing**

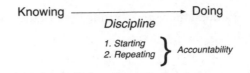

**Figure 6.3  Discipline = Starting + Repeating with Accountability**

In my experience discipline is made up of nothing more than the following two components:

1. **Starting:** The most successful people start a lot.
2. **Repeating:** If it works, and you like it, do it some more. If it's not enjoyable to you, stop it. If the activity is not generating results, adjust it, or replace it with something else that works better.

There's also a third component:

3. **Accountability:** Discipline around new activities is implemented best if somebody holds you to doing what you intend to do (see Figure 6.3). You need somebody to ask you about what you are doing, somebody for you to report to. By the way, it's almost impossible for you to hold yourself accountable. I've learned with clients that for accountability to influence action, it must be external. *You* are too weak of an enforcer on yourself. *You* are too easy to reason with. More on this in Chapter 45.

## How I Lost 50 Pounds in Four Months

I have a herniated disc in my back; it's the lowest one, between my L4 and L5 vertebrae.

It had bothered me for quite a few years, and it was getting worse. One day, I was giving a speech in New York City with about 600 people in the audience. And for the first time in my life, my leg went numb. A minute after that, my lower back lit up with a nerve pain I had not yet experienced. I hadn't experienced either type of pain before, and here, I got to enjoy both in front of all these people.

This happened toward the beginning of my speech, and I was dragging my numb leg around the stage—which is what you want in a speaker, isn't it? I was sweating from the pain, and I was scared, because I didn't know what was happening. I thought maybe the rest of me would start going numb next.

Luckily, I got through the speech, walked out of the conference center, and called my wife.

I told her I couldn't live like this anymore.

I had consulted some of the best doctors in the country about my back.

They told me I had two options: surgery or pain medicine. Neither one was attractive, and I decided I wasn't going to choose either option.

But I knew I had some weight to lose. Since the day my twins were born, I had started gaining weight. I was 6-foot-6-inches and weighed 265.

So, on that phone call with my wife, I told her I was going to try to lose the weight. It couldn't hurt, and even if my back didn't get better, I'd be healthier.

That day, upon returning home, I stopped eating everything besides fruits and vegetables. Like most people, I had tried dieting many times before. I did all the fad diets, and all the trademarked, brand-name diets. The problem has always been that I love to eat. I love the taste of food, and I don't stop eating when I'm full. And I love *all* food. Meat. Carbs. Snacks. Dessert. I do not discriminate. Food is my good, good friend.

But, on that day, the pain and discomfort overcame all of that, and I decided: from now on, natural food only. Food that grows. Fruits and vegetables. *I started.*

I got through the first day, and I thought, "holy cow, I did it."

The next day I woke up and did it again.

*I repeated.*

The weight started coming off. Fast and furious.

I lost 27 pounds in the first month.

I was down 40 pounds after two months.

And after four months and several annoying plateaus, I was down 50 pounds.

People would ask me how much weight I wanted to lose. I would tell them I had no idea, I was going to keep eating this way until I was done losing weight. People would ask how long I would stay on the diet. I'd tell them I didn't know, until it stopped hurting.

I started and repeated, and my wife was my accountability, as she always is. I applied discipline.

*Growing your revenue requires exactly the same approach.*

You start doing something new today.

Tomorrow you repeat it.

The next day, do it again.

After a week or two, assess results.

You can either stop it or continue doing it. If you continue, you can think about adding in another new action. If you stop it, replace it with something else. The good news is that in the next section I will teach you 22 different techniques you can start and repeat. And it doesn't matter one bit which ones you do, only that you *do*.

Two years after I lost the weight, I'm proud to tell you that I've kept it off. I still *mostly* eat fruits and vegetables, with a treat or three mixed in throughout the week.

And, best of all, the weight loss took care of the pain, which is 90% less than what it once was.

Sometimes, the doctors do not know best.

And sometimes, discipline can do what doctors—and, in the world of business, *consultants*—cannot.

What will you start tomorrow?

Will you repeat it?

And who will hold you accountable?

A lot of new revenue—and, perhaps, pain reduction—lays in the answers to these questions.

## Chapter Summary

- You already know most of what I'm about to teach you.
- The question is, are you doing it?
- The distance between knowing and doing is made up of discipline.
- Discipline is made of two parts: starting and repeating.

# 7 | The Mind-Numbingly Simple Definition of Marketing

People often overcomplicate marketing.

We make it nebulous; we make it about branding and social media and advertising and search engines. All of this is fine, and if you are so moved, learn about these areas of marketing. But these are not the efforts that will make you the most money the fastest, which is my singular purpose with this book.

For the purposes of the small and mid-size business, marketing is nothing more than *systematically communicating your value to people who can buy it*.

That's it.

Nothing more.

Do this, and your business will grow significantly.

And since this is a book, and I cannot end the chapter here, even though I've already written the most important sentence you will find in this chapter, let us dig into this definition.

*Systematically* means repeatedly—again and again. It also means there's a pattern to your communication. That is, you're not communicating randomly, but on some kind of schedule. So your newsletter might come every two weeks, and your webinars monthly, and your handwritten note twice a year.

*Communicating* means to clearly explain. For our purposes, we want communication across multiple media: online and offline, the more personal the better. Group communications are fine if you follow my formats, but understand that *everyone* sends mass mail. You should aim at a minimum of an equal balance between group mailings and one-on-one communications. That is, for every mass mailing or newsletter people receive from you, they should hear from you personally, one-on-one, at least once.

*Your value* is what is being communicated. This means you're not systematically communicating about your products and services. Rather, you're systematically describing how customers benefit when they work with you. So, you're talking about how much your business-to-business customers grow sales, expand market share, retain employees, and so on. If you sell to consumers, you're describing how you save them time, money, and all the different ways you improve their lives and benefit their families. Of course, it's okay to mention your products and services here, but they are not the focus of the communication.

*People who can buy from you* are just that: People who can write a check or give you a credit card. In most industries, the more senior the title, the bigger the check they can write. I do a lot of work with manufacturers and wholesale distributors. Many of my clients need to deal with customers in purchasing or influencers like architects or engineers. We must market to these people, and if possible, we should try to include their more senior colleagues like CEOs, presidents, and owners. Basically, this part of the definition identifies *your list*. A good list is made up of as many people who can buy from you as possible.

In order for marketing to generate revenue, you need all four of the elements of my definition in motion. That is, people must hear from you regularly, or systematically. If they don't they'll forget about you in about three seconds. If they hear from your competition more than they hear from you, guess who they'll be buying from? You need to communicate your message using one-on-one methods at least as often as you use company-to-many channels. You need to focus on your value, not your products and services. And you need to deliver these communications to people who can buy from you. It's okay to round out your list with influencers, but they cannot be the core. A core of influencers without senior-level buyers means your list is made up of people who are happy to learn from you and review your information but who cannot buy from you.

## Selling Pushes, Marketing Pulls

It's important to clearly differentiate between selling and the kind of marketing I'm asking you to implement here:

Selling pushes while marketing pulls.

Selling closes while marketing opens.

Selling describes products, services, and prices, while marketing describes how your prospect will be improved after he becomes a customer.

Selling is you moving toward the prospect while the prospect often takes steps backward to keep his distance. Marketing is you drawing the prospect toward yourself by communicating value and demonstrating how his peers have been improved after they've purchased from you.

One final note on the systematic aspect of this: don't be afraid to repeat yourself. Even though you tell prospects about your products and services today, it doesn't mean they'll remember them tomorrow. After all, how many times have you heard, "Oh, you guys do that?!" from someone not long after you told him you do exactly that?

Communicate your value repeatedly and regularly to a good list of buyers.

That's what we're doing here.

That's marketing.

---

### Chapter Summary

The simplest definition of marketing you will ever see: Systematically communicating your value to people who can buy it. That's it. Anything more than this needlessly overcomplicates things, which, by the way, "marketing experts" love to do!

# 8

# The Only Meaningful Measure of Marketing

One of my clients is a wonderful, kind man who is the owner of a very successful firm in the tough print distribution business. When he came to me he was what I call a hypermeasurer. If he couldn't measure it, he wouldn't do it. So in a well-intentioned but misguided effort to measure his marketing, he was focused on tracking the following items:

- Facebook friends
- Twitter followers
- Search engine positioning for various search terms
- Hits, clicks, and page views on his website

Here's the thing about this kind of measuring: For business-to-business companies, which is where I specialize, not one of the statistics just mentioned has any correlation whatsoever with generating additional revenue. More Facebook friends does not equal more revenue. Higher search engine positioning does not equal more revenue. Why? *Because your serious prospects are not looking for you on social media or search engines.* They will, more likely, find you through a referral. Or they will have heard about you.

Or you already know them, because you've called on them, but they have not yet purchased from you. Or, they're already customers, and the goal is to generate more business with them. In all of the examples just listed, the social media–search engine–website statistics have no effect on creating business. And these examples likely account for the vast majority of your current new business efforts.

Can you cite me exceptions? I'm sure you can.

Has your effort on social media or search generated a sale or two? Maybe.

But these are exceptions, and I don't think you should plan your business growth strategy around results that happen rarely, unexpectedly, or accidentally.

Let me close the loop on this: If you sell to consumers, the measurables in the list just mentioned will have slightly more correlation to increasing revenue but not much more.

## Marketing Is as Much Art as Science

One of my business mentors, Alan Weiss, drilled this into my head early on in my career, and he's exactly right: Marketing is as much art as it is science. That is, we must get comfortable with this simple fact: *It doesn't matter which marketing activity generates the next piece of business.* And for many of us in the B-to-B space, it only takes one big hit to make our month, or quarter, or year. So the point is to get the hit.

I've had one client, a machine manufacturer, whose biggest hits come from his following my approaches to effectively marketing at industry trade shows.

Another client, a $100 million distributor, gets the vast majority of his firm's new business by using my techniques for selling more to his existing customers.

And yet another client of mine, a Canadian manufacturer of industrial safety accessories, gets much of his company's new business through powerfully communicating testimonials and case studies to existing customers and prospects.

Everybody's revenue comes from different avenues.

Figure out what yours are by traveling different ones.

If certain avenues generate revenue effectively, travel them more frequently—or send more of your people through them.

If others lead to dead ends, change your route. Try something else.

This is the *art* part of the equation.

You must get comfortable with it. You must try different approaches—all of which are laid out in Part Three—and focus in on the ones that work for you.

## *The Only Marketing Measures That Matter*

Now that we've covered the insignificant measures of marketing, let's discuss the ones that *are* interesting and indicative of success.

New revenue: This is the single most important measure of marketing that there is. How much new top-line revenue is your marketing effort generating for you?

If it isn't creating new revenue, I'm not interested in it.

That's why the popular grad school terms like "brand awareness" don't carry a lot of meaning for me. What if you have great brand awareness that's not generating new revenue for you? What does it matter then? People are aware of your brand, but they're not buying.

To evaluate your marketing, you need to focus in like a laser on revenue generation. Is your company growing as a result of your marketing effort? If it is, you're succeeding. If it's not, you probably need to market more or differently. This is how simple this is.

## Three Additional Useful Measures of Marketing

Here are three additional measures of marketing success. These measures are revenue precursors. That is, they are leading indicators that your sales are about to start moving in the right direction as a result of your marketing. I think you'll find the following three measures useful and indicative of marketing success. And the list is in order—from farthest to closest to new revenue.

## *A Growing List*

I strongly believe that if your list isn't growing, it's difficult for your company to grow. A growing list means more people are constantly being exposed to your value. A growing list means you're reaching more prospective buyers. A growing list means your revenue will soon follow. (More on exactly what kinds of people should be added to your list are discussed in Chapter 28).

### Consistent, Regular Communication

People on your list should hear from you constantly. Communications include one-on-one efforts—like asking the "Did you know?" question and communicating testimonials—as well as company-to-many approaches like sending your newsletter and communicating case studies.

If you promise to send a weekly newsletter, and only deliver it now and then, it would have been better if you didn't start sending it at all. It's critical that people hear from you when they expect it.

### Hand-Raising

The purpose of marketing is to get the people receiving your communications to raise their hands and say, "I am interested in what you are doing." I believe hand-raising is the point where you stop marketing and start selling. It is the transition point between opening and closing. When the prospect raises her hand, she is totally open to your products and services, and now she must be connected with one of your salespeople to earn her business.

As your marketing improves and matures, you want to see increasing hand-raising by customers and prospects. When they do so, they take several steps toward you, and you are there to welcome them with further details about your products, services, and pricing.

---

### Chapter Summary

- Revenue growth is the most important measure of marketing, and all others are very far behind.
- There are, however, three revenue precursors you can use to track your marketing progress:
  - *Your list* must be growing.
  - *Your communication* must be regular.
  - Your customers and prospects are *raising their hands*.

# 9 | It Really Is This Simple!

Not long ago, I was presenting a webinar, one of a series of six that I was commissioned to give by an industry association. This organization shared its member feedback with me. My reviews are nearly unanimously positive after such sessions. But one review struck me after this webinar. This reviewer made it clear he hadn't seen or heard of my work before, even though I had been a keynote speaker and workshop presenter for this association that year. This person also obviously never had a chance to implement my techniques since this feedback was submitted immediately after the session.

In addition to his numerical ratings, this person said, "It can't be as simple as Alex says."

My short response to this person is, "It is *exactly* as simple as I say it is."

Revenue growth occurs when customers and prospects learn about what they can buy from us and how they will benefit when they do so.

So, my approach to growing the companies of my clients centers on getting them to communicate with customers and prospects a lot more. That's really how simple it is.

But now let's take a slightly deeper look at this audience member's feedback.

He wasn't buying that my fast, easy approach would grow his business.

I'm going to assume this person runs a company that's similar to the typical firm in this association. As I describe the typical business in this group, I think we can figure out why this individual feels that growing revenue can't be as simple as I say.

Business isn't easy for him. Never has been.

In fact, business has often been a struggle—a long, often slow slog.

His revenue has been at about the same place for a few years now and shrank quite a bit during the recession.

His is a multigenerational family business. His father may have started it or his grandfather.

He works too hard, and doesn't make nearly enough money for the amount of effort, risk, and time he sinks into his business.

In fact, he'd likely make more money if he went and got a job in his industry. In doing so, he'd lose the risk, too, so life would be *much* easier.

But he can't do that because he has employees, some of whom were with the business when his dad ran it. He feels a responsibility to them and to his family members who ran the business before him.

Plus, he has always aspired to sell the business, and if he just goes and takes a job that dream is out the window. Then all the work, all the struggle, all the running in place, will have been for nothing.

So he stays. He struggles. He works incredibly hard, is fair to his staff, and does well by his customers.

It's easy to understand, then, why my approach seems too good to be true to this man.

Nothing has ever come easily to him.

But my hundreds of clients and thousands of audience members, and tens of thousands of newsletter subscribers who have applied my techniques will tell him this elegant truth: *Communicate your value more, to more people, and more people will buy from you.*

It is not one iota more complex than that.

Tell people what they can buy from you, and what will be better when they do, and they will do so.

And your business will grow—simply, effectively, powerfully, joyously.

---

**Chapter Summary**

It's extraordinarily easy to grow business. Just communicate more with people who can buy from you. That's it. It's no more complicated than that.

# 10 | Your Products and Services Are Much Better Than Your Marketing

I've done work for some of the top consumer electronics brands on the planet: Logitech, TiVo, Lenovo, T-Mobile, and BlackBerry, for example. I worked with these companies when they were at, or near, the top of their respective categories. Even then, their products were so much better than their marketing that it wasn't even close.

I've also worked with some of the most successful, fastest-growing, privately held, small and medium-size companies on the planet. Firms that are $10 million in revenue, $100 million, $200 million, and all the way up to a $2.5 billion closely held organization. When they come to me, all of them, every single one, has products and services that are fabulous, and marketing that is between nonexistent and mediocre.

If you and I were talking right now, and I asked you to describe your products or services, you'd probably go into great detail. You'd tell me all about their various aspects, components, details, measurements, specifications, processes, approaches, and techniques. If I asked you to tell me about your marketing, there would probably an uncomfortable pause, before you'd uncomfortably tell me what you're uncomfortable about when it comes to your marketing. I am able to fairly accurately anticipate our conversation because I've had it many times with your peers—fellow business owners of companies approximately your size. In fact, I often have this same conversation with volunteers in front of large audiences, during role plays.

## Your Products and Services versus Your Marketing

Let's try this exercise, which I think you'll find helpful.

Use the double-axis chart in Figure 10.1 to rate the quality of your products and services, and the effectiveness of your marketing.

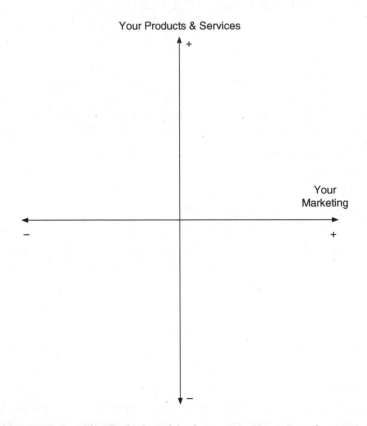

**Figure 10.1 The Relationship between Your Products and Service, and Your Marketing**

### First, Let's Rate Your Products and Services

The vertical axis represents your products and services. On a scale of 0 to 10, with 0 being at the bottom arrowhead, and 10 being at the top arrowhead, how would you rate your products and services? Think about your rating based on these measures: How happy are your customers? How often do they return to you to buy more? How long have they been customers of yours? (If your customers have been with you for 10 or 15 or 23 years, your products and services are probably excellent.) So, rate yourself, and place an X on the vertical axis.

### Now Let's Rate the Quality of Your Marketing

The horizontal axis represents your marketing. In terms of my definition of marketing—systematically communicating your value to people who can buy it—and based on the single most important measure of marketing—new revenue—how would you rate the quality of your marketing? On a scale of 0 to 10, with 0 being at the left arrowhead, and a 10 being all the way to the right, place an X on the horizontal axis.

### How Most Closely Held Companies Rate

I go through this exercise with most of my audiences and every client. So, I've experienced thousands of people responding to these two ratings. Most people rate their products and services at an eight or a nine. They've been in business for many years—sometimes generations—and their customers have stayed with them for decades. Sure, sometimes there are problems, but good firms address them and move on. In my conversations with the customers of my clients, they almost always tell me that problems are to be expected. It's how you respond to them that matters most. It's the responding to these problems that makes up much of the firefighting we spend most of our days engaged in.

Regardless, if your firm is like most successful privately owned small and mid-size companies, your products and services are very, very good. They meet expectations almost always, and your service probably exceeds expectations. The stuff you sell, how you deliver it, and your response to problems is likely terrific.

Now, let's talk about how people respond to rating their marketing. When I ask groups of people, "How good is your marketing, based on the amount of new revenue your systematic communication with customers and prospects generates for you?" this is what I encounter:

> First there is a silence. Frozen silence, too. No movement.
> Then a few people squirm.
> Then I hear some sighs, and some people shake their heads.
> Then some mumbled numbers: three, two, zero, zero-point-two. Can you do a negative rating?
> Once we get past the discomfort of considering the utter ineffectiveness—or nonexistence—of most private companies' systematic, proactive marketing (as opposed to sales) communication with people who can buy from them, we arrive at marketing ratings of between two and three.

### Explaining the Ratings

I've spent a lot of time thinking about why products and services are so much better than the marketing that is supposed to attract buyers for them. This is what I've come up with.

> **The founder or owner is a specialist in the products or services her company sells.** The person running the place was passionate about the products or services when she launched the business.
> **We work to perfect the products and streamline the services, but not the marketing**. Products are designed, sometimes customized, for each customer. Services are changed, adjusted, and customized to each customer.
> **We are culturally and sometimes genetically predisposed against marketing.** This is an interesting one, and a big one. Many people are simply uncomfortable talking about what they're good at. How many times have you heard the statement "We like to let our work do the talking." That's the opposite of marketing. That's modesty. And in marketing, there's no place for modesty.

**We don't know exactly what to do.** As leaders of small and mid-size companies, we know we should market, but we don't know exactly how. Should we be using social media? Advertising? What about search engines? Most industry trade shows have social media experts spouting the benefits of marketing there. There are so many options—and there seem to be new ones popping up constantly.

**We don't have time to market.** In addition to all of the other reasons in this section, we simply run out of time in the day. After addressing customer problems, and meeting with customers, and motivating (baby-sitting?) staff, and driving and flying and planning and spending a bit of time with our families, no time remains for the proactive work of marketing.

**Marketing isn't a priority.** Selling is a priority, but marketing isn't. Making customers happy is a priority. On-time delivery is a priority. Hiring the right talent is a priority. Marketing doesn't make the list. Ironically, tragically, effective marketing will generate more revenue for you than any of these activities. But we don't give it the time it deserves.

### Back to Our Diagram: Next, Find Your Interesting Point

Let's come back to our double-axis chart in Figure 10.1. After you've placed an X on each axis to rate your products and services and your marketing, draw dotted lines from your two ratings to their intersection point. Then draw a star, or whatever symbol moves your spirit, at the point at which they intersect. So, your diagram should now look something like the one in Figure 10.2.

### Identifying the Quadrants

Now, let's take a look at the four quadrants depicted in Figure 10.3.
Starting on the upper right:

### 1. Evangelist Customers

If you have good products and services, as well as good marketing, you will develop evangelist customers. These are people who will do your marketing for you, telling your story to peers of theirs who can buy from you.

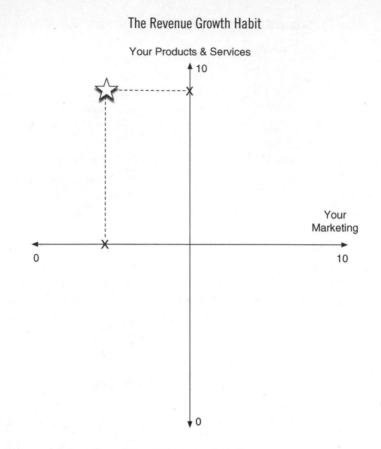

**Figure 10.2 How Most Companies Rate**

Apple has more evangelists than any other company. Consumers who use an iPhone love it and rave about it. Before the iPhone, the iPod had evangelists. Before that, the Mac.

Have you ever talked to somebody who owns a Tesla vehicle? They will corner you, and make sure you cannot escape until you, too, agree to buy a Tesla within 24 hours.

Netflix has evangelists. Amazon, too. And Google has its share also.

These are, of course, some of the top brand names in the world. But you don't have to be well known to develop evangelists in your niche.

For example, I've helped outdoor power equipment companies (think, commercial riding lawnmowers) develop evangelists in their industry, within their region. Similarly, I've helped clients in industries like construction manufacturing, plumbing distribution, and even the pension and benefits industries develop evangelists for their products and services. When you're in

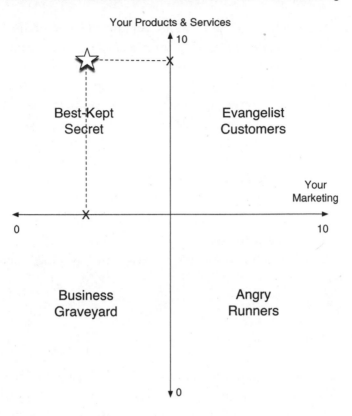

**Figure 10.3   The Quadrants**

the business-to-business space, you don't need to be known internationally. You simply need evangelists within your category or categories of buyers. I have evangelists in all different industries, and a lot of small and mid–size business owners will tell you about the power of my approaches. But the public at large has no idea who I am, and that's just fine with me. It's not about popularity. It's about evangelism in your chosen industry!

## 2. Angry Runners

If you have poor products and services, but good marketing to support them, you have what I call angry runners. These are people who have been convinced to buy your stuff, which isn't any good.

    For an example of a product in this category, think back to when Research in Motion released its first BlackBerry tablet device, the Playbook.

At a time when the iPad and various Android devices dominated the marketplace, RIM released a tablet that didn't . . . do . . . email. You had to download a special app to equip a BlackBerry device for email. They rushed it to the market just to get a tablet into retail. And, of course, they supported their unfinished product with a powerful television marketing campaign. A lot of BlackBerry enthusiasts bought Playbook tablet devices. And, about five minutes after opening their shiny new tablet they were understandably very, very, angry. Many of the Playbooks that were purchased were returned, and the company has yet to recover from its ill-conceived foray into tablets.

Angry runners are the opposite of evangelists: They spread negativity about you to anyone who will listen.

If you're reading this book, it's unlikely you have angry runners as customers.

## 3. Business Graveyard

Companies with poor products and services and bad marketing wind up in the business graveyard, and quickly. These firms don't survive very long. The best examples I can think of here are the vast majority of high-tech start-ups in Silicon Valley, which are mostly backed by venture capital. These companies tend to create products that aren't particularly needed or helpful, and they either have poor marketing or no marketing at all. It's no wonder that the markets these products are aimed at rarely end up hearing about them. Poor products. Poor marketing. Business death. Again, this is not your category, and we don't need to spend any more time discussing it.

## 4. Best-Kept Secret

The vast majority of closely held businesses fall into this category. These are firms with excellent products and services, which you probably have, and less-than-average marketing, which you probably have.

You have wonderful value to offer your market, *but not enough people know about it.*

More people would buy from you, if only they knew about you.

Here's the real mind bender: You are probably a best-kept secret even among your existing customers. That is, they buy what they buy from you, but they don't know what else they can buy from you. The truth is, they would benefit from buying a whole lot more from you than what they're currently purchasing. But they don't know what else you sell, so they cannot buy it.

Good products but poor marketing. This quadrant is most likely where you live.

### New Revenue Is to the Right

Finally, let's take a look at Figure 10.4 and see what it would take to improve our position on this model.

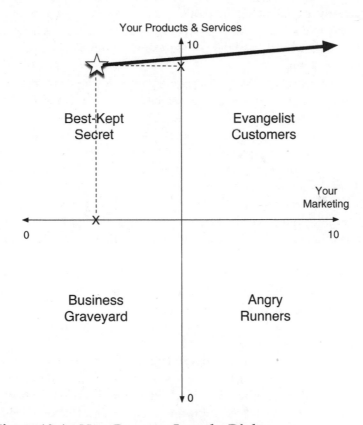

**Figure 10.4   New Revenue Is to the Right**

We want to move from our current position in the direction of the arrow. (Draw an arrow from your intersection point to the upper right of the customer evangelists quadrant.) If we move into the quadrant, we'll attract more customers, increase revenue per customer, and, simply, joyously, make more money.

There are the three key takeaways from this exercise.

1. **The opportunity for improvement is in your marketing.** As you can see, the arrow points hard to the right and slightly upward. That horizontal movement is all marketing. The slight movement from along the product and service axis, from and 8 or a 9 to a 10 will probably not generate much more revenue for you. But an improvement in your marketing will absolutely, positively, unquestioningly create new sales for you.

2. **You're spending your time on an area of your business that's already excellent.** Your products and services are terrific, but your marketing is below average. Here's the key question: Where are you spending more time? Most people would say on products and services not marketing.

    But here's the thing: Your products and services, as they are today, are more than good enough to generate far more revenue for you than they currently do.

    How much additional revenue could your existing products or services generate if you added some simple, effective marketing to the mix? For most small and mid-size companies, the answer is millions of dollars, and for some of them, it's tens of millions. Just think about that.

    I'm not saying you should stop improving your product mix or tweaking your services. Do that if it makes you happy. But understand that your customers are already very happy with what they buy from you. That's why they've been with you for so many years, and that's why they keep coming back. Improving your products and services from an 8 to a 10 would be counterproductive. You would be the only one who would recognize and appreciate that improvement.

    I'm just saying, give me 15 minutes a day to focus on your marketing. Your marketing is the revenue opportunity here.

3. **You don't have to get to perfect.** You don't have to get to the tip of the arrow to generate a lot more revenue for your firm. In fact, you only really need to improve your marketing score by two points or so. If you're at a two or a three, get to a four or five. Just take two steps to the right. Just close the gap between below-average and average. In that

distance, there are millions of dollars. We'll talk about perfection in the last part of this book, but understand that chasing perfection is counter-productive. We just need to get better.

With *The Revenue Growth Habit* you can slightly improve your way to millions of dollars' worth of new sales!

---

**Chapter Summary**

- Most privately held small and mid-size businesses have excellent products and services but ineffective marketing.
- Most of you reading this book lead a business that's probably a best-kept secret—in your market and also among your existing customers, most of whom don't know what else they can buy from you.
- Your products and services are already more than good enough to generate a lot more revenue than you're generating with them now. Improving them is more for you than for your customers or for your top line.
- The low-hanging fruit for revenue growth is in your marketing, where a slight improvement—from below average to just average—will create millions, and, depending on your size, tens of millions of dollars of new revenue for you.

# 11

## "We Don't Like to Brag"

Early in our work together, clients often tell me they have trouble with the boldness required in my approach to revenue growth because "we don't like to brag."

I understand this.

Many of us are raised to value modesty.

After all, how many times did you hear "don't brag!" from your parents growing up?

Communicating why you're good, boldly and widely, goes against what's comfortable. So let me try to help. Here are some of the ways my clients overcome this discomfort.

**You aren't telling people why you're good, your customers are.**
When we go about the process of gathering powerful testimonials from our best customers, we're able to communicate our value in their words. There are myriad reasons this is infinitely more effective than *you* communicating why you're great, but first and foremost is credibility and believability. Your customer is a peer of the prospect's and he's saying you've made him money and saved him time. You capture that quote and communicate it to a prospect of yours. How can the prospect argue?

How can the prospect say it's untrue? Now, if *you* said you're wonderful, and you'll make the prospect money, and you'll save her time, the prospect would have every right to write you off. *Of course* you *say you're wonderful, you're trying to sell to me!* When we put it in the customer's words, it's not bragging. It's simply passing along the truth.

**You're not bragging, you're helping**. Remember, your work helps people tremendously. You improve lives and companies. You save people time and make them money. You make your customers look good to their bosses; you help them make their customers happy and coming back for more. Don't you believe that your customers are far better off working with you than your competition? Then why would you withhold such value from them and the ensuing revenue from yourself? Communicate how you help customers and the money will follow.

**This process is a success loop**. A success loop, by the way, is the exact opposite of a vicious circle. The more you gather testimonials and spread positivity being relayed by your customers, the bolder and more confident you become. When you're bold and confident, you communicate your value widely, easily, and happily. The rate-determining step in the loop, then, is asking for the testimonials. Ask. Listen. Enjoy. Improve. Become bolder. Create confidence. Communicate your customers' improvement in their words. Deposit your new revenue. (One of my greatest pleasures is hearing about clients' growing bank accounts!)

I recently concluded a project with a large manufacturer of industrial protective gear. Two brothers now run the place, which was started by their father. One of the brothers was quite uncomfortable initially with the whole "bragging" aspect of this work. He'd never asked customers what they thought about his company's work before. Nor had he communicated their thoughts and feelings to the world before.

He was hesitant to call customers and ask them for their thoughts and feelings.

But then he did.

And to his great surprise, they were thrilled to hear from him. *The owner is calling me!* Remember, these customers usually deal with outside salespeople, or inside salespeople, or customer service people.

Also, they did not hesitate to share what they loved about working with his firm.

And they thanked him for calling, and caring. *He* was benefiting, but *they* were grateful. Pretty cool, isn't it?

Throughout this project, my client would often joke with me and say, "I can't believe your stuff really works!"

People are constantly surprised at how easy this is.

Your biggest obstacle is yourself.

Get out of your own way, and do what comes naturally to you.

Help people.

And tell your customers and prospects about the amazing ways they'll improve from your help.

That's not bragging.

That's letting people benefit from your great value.

They deserve that, don't they?

---

**Chapter Summary**

- Most prospects don't know the wonderful things you can do for them because you don't communicate it.
- When you share testimonials, you're not bragging, you're letting your customers explain your value.
- You're not bragging, you're helping.

# 12 | Frequently Raised Resistance (FRR)

In this chapter, I'd like to address common questions and points of resistance that are often raised when seeking customer insights, uncovering their positive thoughts and feelings about your work, turning them into testimonials, and communicating them far and wide to your market. These are the primary reasons clients and audience members tell me they don't ask for testimonials and referrals more often. I want to go through these here because they come up consistently, and you may be thinking about one or two of these yourself. Following each point of hesitation, discomfort, or resistance, is my take and feedback.

When I ask clients and audiences why they don't have these conversations, and why they don't ask for testimonials and referrals more, this is what they say.

**I don't want to impose.** You're not imposing, you're striving to help more people. That's your job in the world. Further, have you ever known anyone who didn't wish to share their opinion when asked? I don't know about you, but I've never heard anybody say, "No, I'd rather not tell you my thoughts about that." To the contrary, people are thrilled to be asked for their thoughts and are usually eager to share their feedback. Remember, you're only asking your best customers, and this person is on the very short list. They're honored you're calling them. Handle yourself accordingly.

**What if they don't have anything nice to say? What if they're not as happy as I think they are?** This one is like not going to the doctor because you're afraid of what she'll find. If your customers are not as happy with you as you thought they were, then at least you'll know, and you'll understand what you need to improve. But let me tell you this: If you approach your best customers and ask them for testimonials using my approach, 99% of the time they will give you really good, emotional feedback about your great value.

**What if they reject me and say no?** Remember, you're asking your best customers. In my experience, nearly every one of your best customers will not hesitate to share their positive experiences with you. They are almost always honored you're asking.

**If I post these testimonials on my website, I'll be sharing my customer list with my competition.** Do you think your competition isn't calling on your customers regularly already? And every time they call, your customers make the decision to stay with you. Over and over again, year after year, decade after decade, your customers stay with you. If you share their testimonials, this won't change.

In fact, if you share your customers' testimonials, they are actually less likely to leave you for the competition. They'll feel an additional loyalty to you, since their testimonials are on your website. And if they ever do tell you they're leaving, just say the following with a smile: "Are you crazy, don't you remember all these wonderful things you said about us? You can't leave! You're on our website!" I've actually had clients retain business this way, with my coaching. Their customers agreed!

**I don't have time.** We've covered this one already, but here's a New York version of the kinder, gentler advice from earlier in the book: Do you really not have 90 seconds to 15 minutes a day to grow your revenue by 15% or more? Because I do. And all of the owners and CEOs of my fast-growing clients do. My guess is that you simply don't make the time. Look at your day honestly, and try to tell yourself that you don't have time to send an extra email or ask an extra question or two on an existing phone call once a day.

**I don't know how to ask. I don't know what to say.** You do now, so that's not an excuse any more. You want to ask your customers what they like best about working with you—that's your lead-in for testimonials. And for referrals, just ask them who else they know who would benefit from working with you. That's how easy this is. If they're good customers of yours, they will be happy to help you.

**They won't let me use their names and company names with their testimonials.** I've done thousands of these interviews with the customers of my clients. My experience is that 95% of the time they won't hesitate to allow you to use their names and company names. Four percent of the time, they will ask to see which of their comments you wrote up, which is a fair and reasonable request. So, you'll run it by them first, and they will almost always approve. And 1% will not grant permission. Which means you need to have this conversation with *many* customers before you come across one who will not grant permission.

The reason people are so happy to let you share their thoughts and feelings with the world is because they've just spent 5 or 10 or 15 minutes thinking and speaking positively about you. They're singing your praises, in depth, for an extended period of time. They're on a roll of positivity. *Can we use some of your comments in our materials?* "Why, yes, yes you can."

It's not like everyone they're working with is asking them for their thoughts and feelings. They're not getting these requests daily, or weekly, or monthly. In fact, you're probably the only one who is asking. Think about that. It's a rare and unique request. You care enough to ask. That's a big deal to customers. They value that. Wouldn't you be impressed if the owner of a company you're doing business with calls you personally and asks for your feedback? It's impressive!

**Why would they want to refer me?** Because you help them. And because people are happy to connect their friends and colleagues with good, dependable partners. Think about your own personal life: If you (finally) find a good, dependable, effective, punctual chiropractor, or interior painter, or lawn service, aren't you happy to tell your friends and family about them? Now, that's your personal life, but it's the same in business except we need to ask for those referrals. So, ask!

## What This Resistance Has in Common

Now let's look back at the list of italicized resistance items in this chapter. Together now, these are the reasons people hesitate to ask for testimonials and referrals: You don't want to impose; fear of the customer not having anything positive to say; fear of rejection from the customer; fear of your customers being stolen; you don't have enough time; you don't know how to ask; fear that you won't get permission to use the customers' names; fear that customers won't refer you.

What do these issues have in common? What are they?

They are *self-limiting beliefs.*

In reality, not one of them is true. But you believe them and abide by them, and so you act—excuse me, fail to act—accordingly.

I once had a client—the owner of a distributorship that was over $100 million in revenue when we worked together—who was afraid of calling his customers for their feedback. He thought they wouldn't have time. He thought they'd reject him. He was afraid he would screw it up. Then he phoned one and discovered that the customer was thrilled to talk to him, and, in fact, was honored that the owner had called.

The vast majority of my customers are uncomfortable asking for referrals. Heck, *I* spent a long time being afraid to ask. *What if I screw it up? Why would they want to refer me?* Then I started asking. And my customers started referring. And I've never looked back. Ask.

People who are clinically depressed often create false realities in their minds. That is, they believe people perceive them far more negatively than people actually perceive them. So they go through their days, weeks, and months thinking that they are unliked, unloved, and worse, unlovable. Of course, the reality is that they *are* liked and loved, they just don't realize it.

Self-limiting beliefs hold us back.

Self-limiting beliefs are very strong—foundational even. They are in our cells. Fear of rejection is possibly the greatest foe that success and accomplishment has ever seen. Almost always, fear wins. It's so strong, that it cannot be changed.

If we fear rejection from our customer, we cannot simply sit down at our desk and say, "Today, I will make the call."

The fear will prevent us from doing so.

So, how do we deal with self-limiting beliefs that are so strong?

What can we do about them?

We must blow them up.

We incinerate them.

How?

With a replacement belief that is just as powerful as the limiting one.

Consider: "I help my customers tremendously, and I owe it to my prospects to help them, too."

Or: "I have tremendous value, and my target market deserves to benefit from it."

Create your own.

Write down the *true* belief that will move you to action, destroying the self-limiting belief.

Write it down now. Get a pen, and write in the margin. Go.

Write more than one if you are so moved. You can lean on different true beliefs at different times, using them to overcome different types of internal resistance.

Just remember this: The discomfort with soliciting referrals and positive feedback from customers is ours, not the customers. We are the ones who are uncomfortable with this. Our customers are happy to help us. We must simply allow them to do so.

## Chapter Summary

- Most resistance around gathering testimonials and referrals—which are among the most effective ways we have to grow our business—revolve around fear, usually fear of rejection.
- The reasons that keep us from taking this incredibly important action are self-limiting beliefs. In reality, they are not true. They only exist in our minds.
- Self-limiting beliefs must be replaced with equally strong true beliefs.
- Before you turn the page, get your strong, true beliefs down on paper. Use this page, or any other paper. Take 60 seconds and write down one or two.

# 13 | Your Customers Speak More Positively about You Than You Speak about Yourself

Here's an exercise I often take clients and audiences through.

Get a piece of paper and write down a sentence or two about your company, your products, and services. Answer the questions: What do you do? What does your company do?

Now, think of a good customer. This is a person who has been doing business with you for some time. Think of the person, her priorities, and what her successes and failures consist of. Get yourself into her head—think about what's important to her. Got it? Now, in a couple of sentences, answer these questions from her perspective:

- What are her favorite things about doing business with you?
- How is she improved as a result of working with you?

At this point, most people talk about time saved, trust, dependability, reliability, relationship, and other factors that have nothing to do with products or services. When customers describe you, they talk about the impact of your work, not the work itself.

Now look back and compare your answers and "her" answers.

Which ones have more emotion?

Which ones are more interesting?

Which ones would compel you to learn more about your company?

It's interesting that both descriptions of your company come from *you*. Same person, same brain. When you describe your firm as yourself, it's all about what you do. When you describe your company from a customer's perspective, you talk about your value and how you help people. The latter will generate more revenue for you. The former will commoditize you and make you boring—probably even to yourself.

The fact is, your customers speak more positively about your products and services than you speak about them yourself. This is because they experience your value, while you spend your days responding to customers' issues and concerns. You marinate in your customers' negativity, because that's what comes to you on its own. But the vast majority of your customers marinate in the wonderful value they receive by working with you.

To successfully grow our businesses, we must start thinking about our value more like our customers do. This is one of the great keys to fast revenue growth.

We must begin communicating about ourselves more like our customers do.

We must begin to describe our products and services in terms of their impact on our customers.

Want to know the best way to start thinking about our businesses more like our customers do?

We need to hear them talking about us—as much as possible. We must immerse ourselves into the positive thoughts and feelings of our customers. We must ask them how they are improved by working with us. And then we must listen, absorb, marinate, and simmer.

In the next chapters, I'll tell you exactly how to uncover your value in your customers' words.

**Chapter Summary**

- We tend to describe our companies in terms of our products and services.
- But our customers talk about the value they receive from us.
- When customers describe us, they focus on our relationship, time savings, business growth, trust, dependability, reliability, support, and other emotional factors.
- Our customers speak more positively about us than we speak about ourselves.
- One of the great keys to revenue growth is to start thinking and talking about our companies more like our customers do.

# 14 | Marinating in Positivity

## *The Magic of Proactive Customer Conversations*

The easiest and fastest way to change your mindset is to listen to your customers describe your company, products, services, and value. If, as we established in the last chapter, your customers speak more emotionally, compellingly, and effectively about your firm than you do, then we need to spend time absorbing their thoughts and feelings.

## Customer Complaints Find Us

Unhappy customers bring their concerns to us automatically. We don't need to ask for the negative stuff. It finds us on its own. This is human nature. It's why we are quick to call the restaurant manager over when the waiter hasn't brought us our drinks or food in a timely fashion. (In your customers' world: "It was late! I can't keep waiting for this. My guys are standing around!") But when the waiter is meeting our expectations, we almost never call the manager over to compliment his staff member.

We are wired to complain but say little when things are as we expect them to be.

The problem with this is that the customers with problems (who are the minority) become the squeaky wheels, but the customers who are pleased (the great majority) tend to be invisible. So we spend our weeks hearing from, and servicing, the unhappy customers. We naturally marinate in negativity.

## But We Have to Go Get the Good Stuff

When we talk with happy customers we are exposed to the great positivity with which most of our customers think about us. It serves to counteract the negativity that comes in to us automatically throughout the day.

Here's the thing about getting at the positive thoughts and feelings of our happy customers:

*We have to go get it.*

We need to make time for it, and ask our customers what they like best about working with us.

If we don't ask, they probably won't tell.

And even if they do, say, compliment you in an email, you need to pick up the phone and dig in to their compliment to get at the thoughts and value behind their email. Early in their work with me, my clients often stop at the email, pleased to see something positive come in. But I tell them that we need to understand *why* this was valuable to your customer. What specifically improved for your customer as a result of this good thing happening? How is your customer better off?

Customers rarely call us to tell us what a wonderful job we're doing and to lay out exactly what has improved for them as a result. They rarely call us to tell us how much time or money we've saved them. They rarely tell us, on their own, how we've improved their company or their life.

We have to go get that.

We have to ask them about it.

And they will be happy to tell us.

## A Steady Drip

Customer issues and problems come to us regularly, and we are consistently reacting to, and impacted by, these customers.

As such, we want to create a steady influx of customer-stated value.

One per month isn't enough, because the customer complaints will dwarf that one conversation.

The goal is consistency: A nice, steady flow of information about how your customers are better off as a result of working with you.

## Pouring Cement on Your Relationship

When you ask customers for feedback about their experiences in working with you, you are pouring cement on your relationship with them. You are telling them that it's important enough to you to understand how you're doing for them that you will take time out of your day to ask them about it personally. You are saying, *I care*. And the competition isn't making these calls. You're the only one calling your customer like this. Think about the immense value of that.

Further, in agreeing to talk with you, the customer is pouring cement on his relationship with you. He is taking time out of his day to tell you how he perceives your value. He is spending 10 or 20 minutes complimenting you, thinking positively about you. He is saying, *yes, you may use my comments in your materials*. He is giving you permission to use his name connected to your firm. This customer will likely never leave you.

## What Happens When We Marinate in Positivity?

When we hear the positive thoughts and feelings of our happy customers, our mindset shifts

We think less about our products and services and more about how we improve lives and companies.

We think less about what we need to fix and more about the wonderful ways we help our customers.

We think less about imposing and more about adding value.

Further, when we are consistently exposed to what we do well for customers, we become more bold.

And when we are bold, we are more confident.

We take more action. More things get done.

We don't hesitate to pick up the phone. We never worry about bothering our customers with a call, for they are lucky we have selected them to speak with about the value we bring them.

We don't fear rejection, because the world is full of prospective customers we can help. If this one says "no" then there are thousands of others who can say "yes."

When we are bold and confident, we don't worry, we execute helpful action.

We communicate testimonials.

We ask for referrals.

We ask customers if they know that there are many other things they can buy from us.

We let the world know of our value, and we allow people to take advantage of it and buy it.

When we are consistently exposed to our customers' positive thinking about us, we ask for their business more, because they deserve to do more business with us. We grow the business more.

We are more successful.

Our staff and colleagues make more money.

Our family lives better.

We travel.

Our children go to good schools.

And we eat out at nice restaurants.

When we are bold and confident, life is simply better.

And we are bold and confident when we talk to our customers about what they like best about working with us.

All of this happens when you talk to your customers.

I am proof of this.

My clients are proof.

My audiences are proof.

It really is this simple.

## Chapter Summary

Listen to your customers, absorb their positivity, marinate in it, become bolder, become more confident, take more action, and grow your revenue.

# PART THREE

# 22 Fast, Simple Techniques for Revenue Growth

# 15

# What These 22 Revenue Growth Techniques Have in Common

Now that you know how to *think* about your company, products, services, and value, let's dive deeply into the tools and techniques that will grow your revenue. This part of the book is all about ways to grow your business. I'm going to arm you with you 22 techniques for sales growth in this section. They all share similar traits and characteristics. First, let's talk about what they have in common.

## They Are Communication Actions

All of the approaches I detail here are ways to communicate about your products, services, and value to people who can buy them. These are techniques to tell your customers and prospects about what they can buy from you, and how they will be improved when they do so.

I *will not* be teaching you about improving your graphics or your printing collateral.

I *will* be arming you with different ways—electronic, analog, and the good old-fashioned face-to-face conversation—to tell your customers and prospects about what they can buy and why they should.

## One-on-One and Company-to-Many

As discussed in Chapter 2, some of your communication actions will be one-on-one. These consist of you communicating with customers and prospects directly and personally—by phone, email, postal mail, and in person. But these communications are not only your responsibility, they should be undertaken by all customer-facing staff. That is: management, salespeople, customer service people, and, if you have them, marketing people.

The other type of communication action detailed in this part of the book is of the company-to-many variety. This is mostly list-based communication, where you talk about your products, services, and value to a group, or multiple groups, of customers and prospects. Most of my clients have a single marketing leader who organizes and maintains this type of communication, with significant input from ownership and myself. You now have my input in this book. As an owner or leader of your firm, try to identify the person who is best suited to lead your communication effort. Then, as I do in my projects, start them slowly, with a focus on building and organizing your list (Chapters 28 and 29) and sending a high-value newsletter (Chapter 30).

## A Focus on Quantity, not Quality

In revenue growth, quantity trumps quality. *The more that people hear from you, the more they will buy.* Your revenue is directly proportional to the number of times customers and prospects hear from you. This is, of course, not the case with your products, which have to be exact and precise. But the marketing does not need to be perfect, only helpful. So, in these pages, you will find a wide range of approaches to implement so that your customers and prospects hear from you early, often, and repeatedly.

### 15 Minutes or Less

If you read the opening chapters, you know that I'm not asking you for a day a week.

I'm not even asking for an hour a day.

I am merely suggesting that you tell somebody something about your products, services, or value, once a day. Just one communication action a day is enough.

And this always takes less than 15 minutes a day.

It usually takes 5 minutes or less.

Sometimes this activity is a quick email, made up of you copying and pasting a customer testimonial, adding the words, "Let's talk about providing you with the same value."

Then you send it.

That's it. You've marketed for the day, and you can go back to putting out fires and addressing customer concerns.

## Snowflakes to Blizzards

Now imagine if most of the customer-facing people at your firm performed these quick communications as well. All the salespeople. All the customer service people. All the managers. We'll run through some fascinating numbers during the chapters that follow, but think of each one-on-one effort, each outreach, as a snowflake. In parallel, we have company-to-many communications taking place. Together, these snowflakes add up to a powerful blizzard of marketing, putting you in front of your customers again and again. The best part is, you will be sending information they find valuable, not sales pitches. They will look forward to your communications.

## Like Your Products and Services, These Communications Help People

Your products and services really help people, right? So will these communications. In fact, that's the whole point: To demonstrate your great value to people so that they can either start buying from you, or, if they're already a customer, so that they can buy more.

Just as your products and services help improve lives and companies, your marketing will also. You will be teaching your customers and prospects about how to improve different areas of their work and their companies. You'll be describing how your products and services will save them time and money, and grow their top lines as well. You'll be educating them about all they can buy from you.

With these communications, you won't feel like you're pitching, or selling, or wasting your people's time. So you won't hesitate to pick up the phone, or ask the extra question, or send the extra email. These actions will be seen as valuable. And value leads to revenue.

## These Techniques Are Simple

The techniques in the pages that follow are easy to understand and easy to execute. I've boiled down revenue growth to a series of simple one-step actions that combine to generate serious revenue growth. Complexity will not keep you from taking action.

People tend to overcomplicate revenue growth in small and mid-size companies.

It's not hard.

It's about letting people know about all that they can buy from you and how they will be improved as a result.

That's what we're going to communicate to them.

## No Money Required

Almost all of the methods described here cost nothing.

You don't need money, as most people incorrectly assume, to grow your company.

You need a little personal effort and some personal attention.

That's what I'm asking you for here: Some intentional action, which requires no investment, except for some elbow grease.

## A Focus on Language

Because these are communication actions, they revolve around language. You can apply many of the communications face-to-face, on the phone, or in written form. Many of the chapters that follow will arm you with the words to use to execute the techniques most effectively. Pay attention to the language. Notate it. Make it your own. Language shapes marketing, which shapes revenue growth.

The good news is that we do not need to be perfect with any of this—just good enough. Get it to mostly ready, get it to helpful and valuable, and move it out into the world. *Ship*, as Seth Godin has made a career out of saying. He's right.

## There's No Wrong Way to Do This

You can't screw this up. There's no wrong way to implement this. The goal is to communicate with your customers and prospects more. Just let people hear from you more, and they'll buy from you more. *How* you choose for them to hear from you is entirely up to you. Everything you try is the right thing. There's no wrong thing. There's no wrong way. We're just helping people more.

## Do What You Like, Do What Works

There are 22 revenue growth techniques in this part of the book. You don't need to do all of them. You don't even need to do some of them. And in fact, I don't even care which ones you do.

Pick one that sounds good to you, and try it. If you like it, and it generates some positive results, double down on it and do it some more.

If you don't like it, you'll have trouble getting yourself to do it, so stop trying, and move on to something else.

If you know you hate writing, avoid those efforts.

If you like speaking, look for opportunities to apply these techniques that way.

If you hate making calls, you probably shouldn't be in sales, but even so, try the approaches that involve writing and talking face-to-face.

*All* of the approaches in this section can grow your business. But *any* of them is good enough to start with.

So as you read this part of the book, identify the approaches that feel good to you. Then try them, understanding that the trial is, by definition, temporary and open for analysis and adjustment.

Do what you like. Do what works.

And the revenue will follow.

---

**Chapter Summary**

- The revenue growth techniques outlined in this book are communications actions, both one-on-one, from you to a customer or prospect, and company-to-many, from you to lists of customers and prospects.
- These approaches are fast, free, and simple. They require no more than 15 minutes a day, and often just moments.
- This marketing work is designed to help customers and prospects, just as your products and services do.
- Focus on the approaches that work, and the work you like. If you dislike a particular approach, don't do it anymore. It doesn't matter which of these communication techniques you use, only that you communicate with your customers and prospects systematically.

# 16 | Choreographing Your Revenue Growth Dance

This part of the book contains 22 techniques to grow your business.

Some of them are designed to be implemented one-on-one by your customer-facing people, and some of them are to be communicated by the company, to your list. And some techniques, like communicating testimonials and case studies, can be done on either track.

Your job as the implementer of this process at your company is choreography.

You want every dancer taking the right steps, moving in the right direction, synchronized with everybody else.

So, here is some detail on the organization and order of execution:

1. **First, review the various one-on-one techniques with your colleagues, and let people select what they'd like to do.** We don't care what they do, as long as they execute one of the one-on-one techniques in this section daily.
2. **Think about what one-on-one communication you can automate.** For example, can you add testimonials to your quotes or proposals, so they appear automatically? Can you have your IT person add testimonials or a "did you know question" to your email signature?

The more one-on-one communication is automated, the more of it gets out.

3. **Next, gather or review your list, and make sure it's in good shape.**
4. **Your first company-to-many action will be to send a good newsletter, as discussed in Chapter 30.** This should go out every two weeks.
5. **It's important to start the newsletter at about the same time your people start their one-on-one actions,** because we want customer-facing staff to benefit from the newsletter, just as we want the newsletter's effectiveness to be enhanced by the one-on-one communication.
6. **Your newsletter should be the *only* communication happening on the company-to-many track until you're comfortable with your ability to write a good one quickly and regularly.** I repeat: At first, your newsletter is the only thing being sent to your list. Once you get it going well and consistently, you can add additional communications to your list like testimonials, case studies, white papers, webinars, videos, and so on. Master the newsletter first. It's the most important piece of list communications you can execute. By far.
7. **Track results, especially of the one-on-one work.** We'll talk more about this in the next section, in Chapters 44 and 45.

With these specifics in mind, go through the rest of the chapters in this section, and identify the techniques that feel good to you. Think about which ones you might enjoy doing, and which ones may be successful.

Then, try some of them—one at a time.

That's how easy this is.

Ready?

Fire!

(And worry about aiming later.)

---

## Chapter Summary

- Ideally, all customer-facing staff undertakes this communication action.
- Your job is to choreograph the one-on-one action along with the company-to-many techniques.
- A "marketing quarterback" should run the company-to-many communications track.
- Master your newsletter first before adding other communications to the company-to-many track.

# 17 | Growth Technique #1: The Art and Science of Getting the Testimonial

To change our mindset, we must go out and talk to our happy customers. This is how.

## Telephone Is Best

Don't ask these questions by email, because you want the ability to *hear* the customer's voice and to follow up on his questions.

Having this conversation in person is okay, but it makes it challenging to take good notes. You can if you're comfortable with it, but . . .

Telephone is best for these conversations.

You can follow up.

You can listen and take notes.

And you can record the call if you wish.

## Five or 10 Minutes, No More

You're going to average about one testimonial per minute. Which means you don't need to interview your customers for a half hour or an hour.

You need 5 to 10 minutes to ask the questions I will outline shortly. Make it easy for them to agree to give you feedback. Five to 10 minutes is non-threatening and difficult to decline. Go short, and the end result will take you a long way toward new revenue!

## The Good Customers, not the Angry Ones

Remember, we have these conversations with our good customers, not our small, or frustrated, or angry, or "fly-by" customers who move from one lowest price to the next, regardless of the relationship. You have these conversations with your longest-tenured customers, and your most passionate customers, and your largest customers by revenue. But if you have a happy smaller customer, reach out to that individual for a brief conversation, too. It can't hurt, and it only helps.

## Setting Up Your Customer Conversation

There are two easy ways to get your happy customers' thoughts and feelings.

### Option 1: Schedule the Conversation

Identify your top 10 (or 5 or 23—it doesn't matter) customers.

Send them a simple email that reads something like this:

"I'm reaching out to our very best customers, and you're on the short list. We're working on improving how we serve you, and also how we talk about what we do. I would value your experience and feedback on working with us. Do you have 10 minutes to speak with me on Thursday morning? Just looking for your take on how we're doing. It would be a great help to us. Thank you very much in advance."

It's an incredibly flattering, no-pressure setup. The vast majority of the people you send this to will accept.

### Option 2: Add on to Existing Conversations

You talk to customers every day, right?

Add this "positive feedback" chat to the end of your existing conversations:

"Hey, Tom, do you have 5 or 10 more minutes? You're one of our best customers, and I'd like to ask you for your feedback on doing business with us. We've been working together for a long time, and it's important to me to understand how we're doing for you. Can I just ask you a couple quick questions now?"

Again, you're making the customer feel good with this request. Sure, you're asking for a favor, but you're complimenting the customer in the process.

Nearly *everyone* you set the conversation up with this way will accept.

## Starting the Conversation

Start your call by framing the conversation in positivity:

"As I said, I'm having this conversation with just a few of our very best customers. I'm looking for your take on how we're doing, and what's better for you as a result of working with us. There are absolutely no right or wrong answers. You can't tell me the wrong thing. Sound okay?"

Your customer will say yes.

## Permission to Record

This simple question is so important, it gets its own section. We must ask permission to record the call:

"By the way, is it okay with you if I record the call?"

Nearly everyone—and I'm talking 995 people out of 1,000—will say yes.

Then, remember to click on your recorder.

Here's how I do this.

I make the calls through Skype on my computer. I use a plug-in recorder made by a company called Eccam. The software is called Call Recorder for Skype (creative, right?). You can download a free trial at www.ecamm.com and buy it outright for just under $30. I have a good headset that I use, and nobody knows I'm not on a telephone.

I set it up this way because once the recording is finished, it's already on my computer. Then I convert it to an MP3 file via a simple tool included with the call recording software, and I can easily email or otherwise share the audio files with my clients. You can similarly share your call recordings with your staff, managers, or colleagues.

Order is important here.

First, set up the call, using the language in the preceding section. Make your customers comfortable with what you're doing. Then get permission to record, and, ideally, *record the permission*. So, start the recorder, then ask for permission so you capture it.

## Note-Taking

The recorder is running, so you don't *need* to take notes, but I prefer it. I take notes because I can go through them faster than I can review the recording. I also find written notes more convenient to read through and covert into testimonials.

That's the point of these conversations: To turn them into written testimonials and case studies. So try to take good notes while talking with your customers.

Your written notes will also serve as a backup to your recordings, in case a technical glitch occurs.

## Key Questions and Follow-Up Techniques

Start with this simple question: "What are you some of your favorite things about working with us?"

The customer will probably quickly identify two or three major areas of value. He might say things like:

- You always deliver on time.
- I can always reach somebody.
- I know that when I ask you to do something, I never have to worry about it again.

These are common examples. The customer could say any one of countless different things he enjoys best about working with you. Think of the customer's two or three items as threads, and your job is to pull on them. Unwind the spool by digging into each item. You want to get at how the customer improves as a result of each item of value he has brought up, and why that is important to him.

So, as if you are having lunch with a friend, start asking follow-up questions:

"That's interesting. Why is it important to you that we deliver on time?"

"How are you improved when we deliver on time?"

You probably know the answer to these questions, but that doesn't matter. We need the customer saying the words, and his name attached. It doesn't matter that you can tell me it will make customers happy when you deliver on time. What I need, as your prospect, is for your customer, my peer, to tell me that *his* customers are happier because you always deliver on time. See the difference? *You* are selling. Your customer is merely sharing his experiences.

I've done thousands of these calls, and I know what the customers of my clients are going to say every time. I can tell my clients almost word for word what their customers will say in response to my questions. But that doesn't matter. To change my clients' behavior, and to arm them with powerful marketing tools, I need them to hear it from their customers. I need testimonials with names and companies attached.

And so do you.

### Quantify Everything You Can

If the customer says you save them time, ask them to estimate how much time. If they aren't sure, ask them to take a guess. If you ask them, they will take a guess. And here, again, it doesn't matter that the number is exactly correct and accurate. The customer is saying it, so it's the truth.

If the customer says you help to save them money, ask them how much money they estimate they've saved with you as compared to their average supplier or partner.

If the customer says you've helped to grow their business, ask by how much. "How much of your revenue would you guess comes as a result of working with us?"

The word "ballpark" is very helpful. We're just looking for an approximation. Just an idea.

### Emotionalize

We want the customer's thoughts and emotions.

"Working with us saves you an hour a day? [Quite a common response!] Wow! That's amazing. What do you think about that? How does that make you feel?"

If this feels uncomfortable to you, that's normal. Just remember that *you* are probably much more uncomfortable with this conversation than your customer is. Your customer has probably thought about all of this already.

### Ask Your Customer to Describe Your Company

Here's a great way to hear how your customer would market your company. Ask him, "If you were talking with somebody like yourself at a different company, how would you describe us? What would you say about us to a person in a similar position at a similar company?"

They will often talk about things like integrity, dependability, relationships, timelines, and many other incredibly value characteristics.

### Three Emotional Words

This is a great question to end with: "What are the first three feelings that come to your mind when you think about working with us."

Terrific question that's totally open-ended and lets the customer take it where he wishes.

Listen carefully, then follow up and ask him why he chose those interesting words.

### Follow Up a Lot

Throughout this conversation, your job is to be present. Really listen. Hear what your customer is saying.

And ask a lot of follow-up questions.

If your friend told you something incredibly interesting at lunch, you'd follow up and dig into her comment, right? Do the same thing here.

Ask, "Why did you say that?"

"Why is that important to you?"

"How does that help you?"

"How are you improved by that?"

Sometimes I follow up on a statement five different ways.

## What Your Customer Doesn't Talk About

I can have this conversation with your customers without knowing anything about your business. *That's because we're not talking about your products and services.* In these testimonial conversations, your customers will not speak about your products and services at all. They will speak about your value, their improvement, your relationship, and the care you take of them. They will talk about how they're better off by working with you. They will not talk about the details of what you sell.

This is a huge reason I want you to talk with your customers, because I want you to experience what they consider important. And it ain't your wares. That stuff is a commodity. Your customers talk about the thing that makes you singular: your incredible value, as they perceive it.

## Obtaining Permission to Share Testimonials

Once you have what you need, bring the call to a close, and ask what is probably the most important question in this entire chapter:

"Thank you very much for your insights and feedback. They're incredibly helpful and valuable to us. I'm grateful for your time. *Is it okay with you if we use some of your comments in our materials?"*

As discussed earlier in this book, 95% will agree, 4% will ask to review the comments first, and 1% will say no.

This is the only permission you need to use your customers' testimonials publicly, *with their name and company.* You don't have to ask again. If you do, and it's days or weeks following your conversation, there's a significant chance they'll decline. Once they've given you permission, the only reason to ask again is your own insecurity. Remember, you are less comfortable with this process than your customers are. You're less comfortable asking for positive feedback than your customers are giving it. Don't project your discomfort onto your customers. You have their permission to use their testimonials. Go and do so.

Now, if, for example, you put a customer's testimonial on your website and she asks you to take it down, do so immediately, no questions asked.

If a customer tells you that you may not use his testimonial publicly, ask if you can share it privately. "May I email your testimonial to a carefully selected prospect of ours privately?"

If your customer says no, ask if you may use his comments anonymously, because even this is more valuable than not using testimonials at all.

## There Is No Wrong Way of Doing This

I'm giving you some very specific questions and approaches here.

Understand this: Yes, there is a correct, precise way of having these conversations.

*But at the same time, there is no wrong way of doing this.*

Listen to your customer, simmer in their experiences, perceptions, and compliments.

Allow it to soak in, and really think about how positively they perceive you.

So what if you don't emotionalize and quantify everything?

So what if you don't do it exactly right?

The important thing is that you allow your customers to describe what they like best about working with you. You capture their thoughts. And you secure their permission to share their thoughts.

That's what matters.

---

### Chapter Summary

- The key question to gathering customer testimonials: "What are some of your favorite things about working with us?"
- The answer will present you with threads to unwind.
- Listen to your customers' answers, and simply be present.
- Ask follow-up questions. Why? How does that help you? What improves for you when we do that?

# 18 | Lessons from a Sample Customer Interview

This chapter contains a transcription of an actual customer testimonial conversation that I conducted on behalf of a client. This interview was conducted within a few months of writing this book. I've generalized and changed identifying facts to protect this generous and helpful customer and my client. My annotations are in italics below.

## The CEO and Owner

This man, let's call him Tom Johnson, is the owner and chief executive officer who orders regularly from my manufacturing client. Tom uses my client's equipment in many of his company's jobs. Let's call my client X Co. Tom is constantly under pressure from his customers. So, when something is late or incorrect with his order from his manufacturers, he gets hammered by his customers, whose jobs are held up. In turn, he comes down hard on his manufacturers. It's a high-pressure job. He has kindly agreed to be interviewed about his experiences with X Co.

I make it clear that I'm calling on behalf of X Co., my client, but this conversation wouldn't look very different if the owner the company asked the same questions.

> **Me:** Tom, thanks for your time. I really appreciate it. As you know, X Co. is only talking with our best customers, and you are on the very short list.
>
> **Tom:** Oh, great, thanks, I have no idea how we got there!
>
> **Me:** We're trying to improve our service, and also how we talk about what we do. As you know, equipment manufacturing isn't the sexiest industry in the world, and the best way I know how to improve is to talk to you and get your feedback. So that's what we're doing here. I'm just looking for your take and experience, and there are no wrong answers. You can't tell me the wrong thing. We'll talk for 10 minutes or so, and I'll get you off the phone. Sound okay?
>
> *Note: I'm setting things up simply and painlessly. I'm also getting a quick, small, easy yes up front.*
>
> **Tom:** Sure.
>
> **Me:** Great. Okay with you if I record the call?
>
> **Tom:** No problem at all.
>
> *Note: Again, a quick, easy yes on the heels of the earlier yes. A pattern of yesses. Out of thousands of these customer interviews, I can count the total number of people who have declined being recorded on two hands. A reminder that you should start the recorder at the beginning of the conversation, so as to capture the permission.*
>
> **Me:** We've been working together for a long time, Tom, and I appreciate your business very much. What has kept you with us so long? What are some of your favorite things about working with us?
>
> **Tom:** The main thing is that your regional sales rep is here four times per year. He is considered a good friend of everyone here. We sit down and we talk about products and our business.
>
> *Note: That's a nice surface-level answer and typical of how these things start normally: logically, not emotionally. Now let's dig into it.*
>
> **Me:** Why is that important?
>
> **Tom:** Well, behind the rep is a company that does what it says. You're responsive to my requests. Everything that happens in our industry is a burning priority. It's important to us to have a company that responds when they say they will. You ship products when you say you will. And you have very few callbacks. I would give you a gold star in all of those areas.
>
> **Me:** How many suppliers do you deal with, Tom?
>
> **Tom:** Fifty total.

**Me:** And where does X Co. rank among those 50 in areas like responsiveness, availability, shipping timeliness . . . the areas you were just talking about?

*Note: See how I set up the question? I want to know where my client ranks in the areas Tom where was just effusively praising them. I know it will be high before he says it.*

**Tom:** You are on top of our list of 50 suppliers.

**Me:** Interesting. What puts us there?

**Tom:** You have done a very good job in getting a very wide product offering that somebody like me needs. We have to have the bullets in our gun to go to market and solve issues for our customers. And X Co. puts those bullets in our gun.

**Me:** Cool, loading the gun! How do we do that?

*Note: The question I ask here almost doesn't matter. I just want him to keep saying nice things about my client.*

**Tom:** X Co. really innovates. You're always adding new products. Several times you've actually introduced new ideas to us that we hadn't even thought about. As a result it leads to us getting the sale, and solving issues that somebody else isn't even able to solve.

**Me:** So we help you sell stuff you wouldn't have sold otherwise? Does that mean we help to grow your business?

**Tom:** Yes, X Co. helps grow my business. Here's our simple formula: We need to connect the group of people buying our product with the group of people that's supplying the product. When we can do that with more types of product, we get really, really good results. The fact is that X Co. helps us handle more work and helps us make our customers look really good.

*Note: How cool is that?! X Co. not only makes Tom look good, but this company helps him make his customers look good. That's invaluable! Now, let's try to quantify it.*

**Me:** That's great to hear. I'm curious, how much would you say we grow your business?

**Tom:** Oh, that's hard, I wouldn't know.

*Note: Don't give up. Plant your feet, and ask again. Make it easy for your customer to answer this question.*

**Me:** Ballpark. I don't need exact numbers. Nobody's going to audit you. How much new revenue do you think working with us accounts for?

**Tom:** If I had to put a number on it, I'd say 23%.

**Me:** So working us accounts for 23% of your new revenue?

**Tom:** Yes, I think that's fair to say.

**Me:** Annually?

**Tom:** Yes.

*Note: What a great testimonial! "Working with X Co. accounts for 23% of annual revenue growth!"*

**Me:** Have you ever thought about it that way before?

**Tom:** No, actually.

*Note: We already knew the answer to that, but it sets up this next question.*

**Me:** What do you think about this? How does it make you feel?

**Tom:** I think that's pretty awesome, don't you? One of my 50 partners accounts for 23% of my total growth! That's amazing.

**Me:** Partner is an interesting word. Do you think of X Co. as a vendor or a partner?

**Tom:** Definitely as a partner.

**Me:** What's the difference?

**Tom:** A vendor just sells you product. A partner cares about you. A partner is interested in your profitable growth and does what he can to help you attain that growth. A partner knows you and your company and your products and your customers.

**Me:** That's great. And X Co. does those things for you?

**Tom:** Absolutely. X Co. is so much more than a vendor to us. You're a partner and a friend.

**Me:** Wow, what makes you say friend?

*Note: I'm just listening and following up. Just like having a drink with a friend. Be present, hear what your customer is saying, and follow up a lot. That's all this is. It's extraordinarily easy to do.*

**Tom:** Look, we've been buying from you for 25 years. I know the owners and their families personally, and they know me and my family. We have dinner together. I'm happy to spend time with them. We are friends. And that's a rare thing in business.

**Me:** Thanks Tom, that's terrific stuff. Let me ask you this: If you were talking with a peer of yours, an owner of a similar company in a different region, somebody who doesn't compete with you but does what you do somewhere else, how would you describe us? What would you say about us to this person?

*Note: This is me asking the customer to market X Co. for me. I want to know what language he'll use.*

**Tom:** I'd say that if you want a quality product, delivered on time, and want to be supported by great people who are honest, caring, and responsible, you should work with X Co. I'd give you my highest recommendation.

**Me:** That's great, thanks.

**Tom:** And you know, I want to say that X Co. is just there for us. That's not to say there aren't problems, because you have problems with everyone, but X Co. steps up and solves them. You don't look for the easiest solution. You look for the right solution, even if it costs you more money or time. You do the right thing, every time. And many times you do it before we ever ask for it. You just do it on your own. And that's a big deal.

*Note: He volunteered this information, I didn't ask for it. This is a common occurrence in the middle of these conversations, once the customer is in a good rhythm and has really dug in to thinking about his experience. Even so, let's help him go even deeper.*

**Me:** So what is that, Tom? Is that peace of mind?

**Tom:** Absolutely. I know that when I place an order with you, I will never mislead my customer. You always deliver to us, which helps us deliver to our customers.

**Me:** How does working with X Co. help you in your job, Tom?

**Tom:** You help me make my customers happy. Not only that, but you help make my customers' customers happy.

**Me:** And what does that mean to you?

*Note: You can't ask this question enough.*

**Tom:** It's wonderful. It's trust. It's warm-and-fuzzy feelings.

*Note: Yes, even tough, experienced, highly-technical customers say this!*

**Me:** Coming up to the end here, Tom, last couple questions. Really appreciate your time and everything you're sharing with me so far. Here's the question: What are the first three emotional words that come to your mind when you think about X Co.?

**Tom:** Oh boy, emotional?!

*Note: That's the reaction more than half of the times I ask this question, which I do in every interview.*

**Me:** Yes, anything that comes to your mind. Don't think too long.

**Tom:** Okay. Well . . .

Reliable.

Friendship.

And just good people.

*Note: They're self-explanatory, but it doesn't hurt to follow up on one of them, if you haven't dug into it yet.*

**Me:** Wonderful. Those are terrific. Why did you say good people?

**Tom:** Well, it's like we've been talking about it. I know they have my back. I know they won't let me down. And I know they'll deal with any problems we may run into.

**Me:** Tom, thank you so much for you time. I really appreciate your insights and feedback, they're extraordinarily valuable to us.

**Tom:** You're welcome, happy to help.

*Note: After the thank-you, always ask for permission to use your customer's amazing comments.*

**Me:** Is it okay with you if we use some of your comments in our materials?

**Tom:** [Without one iota of hesitation] Sure. I would hope you do!

## Lessons from This Customer Interview

Now, let's review the major takeaways from this interview.

### *This Customer Is Like Most of Your Other Good Customers*

An interview this positive is not the exception. It is the norm.

I've done thousands of these, and I ask my clients to let their best customers know I'll be calling. And when I call, this is how the interviews go, almost without exception. They vary in language and adjectives, not in positivity. *If you ask the questions I'm asking, you will get the same kinds of answers!*

This is how most of your customers think of you.

And these are the kinds of testimonials they'll give you.

### *Your Customers Are Happy to Provide This Information*

When you have these conversations, one of the things that strikes you immediately is how easily and naturally customers provide the information. You're just having a nice conversation. They're not struggling to come up with these compliments. Rather, they flow freely, naturally, and happily. The customers are honored you're asking, that you've selected them. They're happy to share what's on their minds. They've thought about all of this before, even if they haven't communicated it to you.

Do not feel like you are imposing on your customers when you ask them to speak with you for this positive feedback. They are impressed that you are making the effort, and they will be pleased to take 5 or 15 minutes out of their day to share their thoughts with you.

### *What Is This Customer Not Talking About?*

Go back through the interview, which is basically a word-for-word transcription of a recent interview I did for a client (but representative of nearly all interviews I do with owners of companies who buy from my clients). What is Tom *not* talking about?

Products.

Services.

Specifications.

Technologies.

Rather, he talks about relationship, friendship, dependability, reliability, and availability.

That's what you should talk about, too.

### *Try to Speak about Your Value More Like These Happy Customers*

The more you hear this kind of happy feedback, the more you will absorb it—intentionally and through osmosis, as it seeps into your brain, both the conscious and unconscious parts. Tom, the customer in the sample interview, speaks the truth about X Co.'s value. He has no reason to lie. He's voting with his money, which he keeps spending with X Co. You focus on your products and services, but your happy customers focus on the value you deliver to their company and also to them personally. Your customers focus on how you improve their companies and their lives. You must shift your focus, and your communication, to these same areas. They are far more interesting, compelling, resonant, and powerful than your products and services.

### The Testimonials

These are the testimonials I would take out of the interview and present to my client to use far and wide:

- "Our X Co. sales representative is here a lot, and he's considered a good friend of everyone here. We sit down and frequently talk about products and our business."
- "X Co. is a company that does what it says. They're responsive to my requests, respond when they say, and have very few callbacks. X Co. gets a gold star in all of these areas!"

- "Out of 50 total suppliers, X Co. is right at the top of our list."
- "X Co. has done a very good job providing the very wide product offering that we need. X Co. puts the bullets in our gun, which we need to go to market and solve issues for our customers."
- "X Co. really innovates. They're always adding new products. Several times they've actually introduced new ideas to us that we hadn't even thought about. As a result, X Co. helps us get the sale and helps us solve issues for our customers that somebody else isn't even able to solve."
- "X Co. helps to grow our business. They help us handle more work and help us make our customers look really good."
- "Working with X Co. accounts for 23% of our annual revenue growth! I think that's pretty awesome, don't you?"
- "X Co. is definitely a partner to us. A vendor just sells your product. But a partner cares about you. A partner is interested in your profitable growth and does what he can to help you attain that growth. That's what X Co. does for us."
- "X Co. is much more than a vendor to us. They're a partner and a friend."
- "I consider the people at X Co. my friends, and that's a rare thing in business."
- "X Co. is just there for us. They step up and solve problems. They don't look for the easiest solution, but the right solution, even if it costs them more time or money."
- "X Co. does the right thing, every time. And many times, they do it before we even ask for it. They just do it on their own. And that's a big deal."
- "X Co. is wonderful. I trust them. Working with them brings me warm-and-fuzzy feelings."
- "When I think of X Co. I think of reliability, friendship, and just good people."
- "I know X Co. has my back. I know they won't let me down. And I know they'll deal with any problems we may run into."

## Reviewing the Testimonials

Here are the top takeaways about turning a customer conversation into these kinds of testimonials.

**A short chat results in a lot of testimonials.** The interview detailed above took no more than 15 minutes in real time. It generated 15 pretty excellent and powerful testimonials. That is one per minute. That's a good ballpark for you to aim for. So, if you talk to a customer for five minutes, expect five good testimonials to result.

**Keep them brief.** A good testimonial can be one or two sentences. It doesn't have to be a paragraph. It *can* be, but I find you may lose the readers' attention. So, keep them tight, maximizing the number of testimonials you create from each conversation. Remember, with testimonials, as with all marketing, quantity is the goal.

**Some liberties are acceptable.** Don't worry about keeping the wording exactly as it was stated to you. While you must keep the *meaning* precisely as the customer communicated it to you, you may take some liberties with language. For example, you may combine sentences from different parts of the conversation, if they make sense together. You may clean up the language and grammar for your customers. Help them sound smart. You can see how my final testimonials above were pulled from the interview. Almost none of them are 100% what the customer said. But all of them are 99% of what the customer said, with small tweaks, combinations, and edits by me. The meaning must be the same, but the sentence structure, and very selectively, the language, can be improved. Out of thousands of these kinds of interviews, a client's customer has never complained about my tidying edits. After all, they said everything that I quote!

**What can you say that's better than this?** There nothing you can say about your company that's more effective than these incredibly valuable testimonials. There's nothing *I* can say about your firm that's better. The words of our happy customers are our most powerful marketing language. And besides that, you get the wildly important value of understanding how your happy customers think about you, and, eventually, you will begin to think about your value more like your customers do!

**In terms of revenue growth, there are few better investments of your time than these kinds of customer interviews.** Spend 10 to 15 minutes listening to a customer sing your praises, and generate 10 to 15 powerful testimonials. Pretty good ROI on your time, right?

In the next chapter, we will go through the various places you can communicate these terrific testimonials.

## Revenue Language: Testimonials

One of these is enough to get you two or three major threads to pull and unravel from the spool.

*The Big Questions*

- What are some of your favorite things about working with us?
- What do you like best about working with us?
- We've been working together a really long time; what has kept you with us so long?

Later in the conversation, try asking these questions:

- How many suppliers do you have in all? Where would you rank us among them?
- How would you describe us to a peer of yours—somebody who is in a similar position at a different company? What would you say about our company to make that person say, "Wow, I really need to work with them!"?
- Does working with us help to grow your company?
- Does working with us help you save time?

*The Follow-up Questions*

Listen to what your customer is saying—really listen—and follow up with a variety of these questions:

- That's interesting, why did you say that?
- How does that help you in your job?
- Have you ever thought about it that way before? How does that make you feel?
- How?
- Why?
- Tell me about that . . .

*Quantifying Questions*

When a customer says you save them time or money ask:

- Let's try to quantify it. You said that working with us helps to save you time. How much time would you guess?
- How much faster is it to work with us than with your typical supplier?
- I love that we help grow your business. If you had to take a shot at it, how much revenue has working with us accounted for?

## Chapter Summary

- Your customers love doing business with you. Your job is to get them to explain why.
- Every time the competition calls, your customers have to decide to stay with you. Their reasons for working with you are well detailed in their heads. Your job is to get them to explain these reasons.
- Note what your customers talk about (value) and what they do not talk about (products, services, pricing).
- Talk more like your customers, and your business will grow.

# 19 | Growth Technique #2: Don't Be a Tree Falling in the Forest— Communicate Testimonials

Now that you know all about the easy conversations that create new testimonials, let's talk about what to do with them.

It doesn't matter if you've collected countless testimonials or even if your website is plastered with them—if nobody is seeing them.

Testimonials, like celebrities, are only as good as the number of people seeing them.

Here's another metaphor: Your unseen, unread testimonials are trees falling in the forest. If nobody sees the incredibly powerful words of your customers, it's as if you never obtained the testimonials to begin with.

What should you do with your customer testimonials?

That's easy: You should communicate them to people who can buy from you—as much as possible, in as many formats as possible. And don't forget to communicate your wonderful testimonials *internally*, to your staff, as well.

## Communicating Testimonials Internally

As detailed in Chapters 17 and 18, when you let your staff and colleagues experience the amazing endorsements of your customers, their thinking changes about the company, and their action levels go way up. They become bolder, more confident, and take more action (Figure 19.1).

Here are some easy ways to communicate testimonials internally to change mindsets and behavior.

**A weekly note from the president.** One of the most powerful mindset changers my clients implement is a regular, simple, short email from the owner to all the staff. This note has two items: a testimonial, and a sentence or two on what to take away from this testimonial. It's a way to "focus on what we're good at," as one client told me recently, "because we tend to lose sight of that."

**Monthly sharing of audio recordings.** One of my clients likes to play one complete audio recording from my conversations with his customers at every staff meeting, which occur monthly. His staff sits, transfixed, almost mesmerized. He told me early on that he has never seen his staff so focused and engaged in anything *he* has ever told them! Let your people hear the entire conversation, and experience how easily it flows, how happily your customers share their kind words, and how pleased they are with your team's work.

**Circulate a book of testimonials.** Collate all testimonials from customer insight calls into a single document and circulate it, in hard copy, to everyone. You'll find that it sits on people's desks. It will be a prized professional resource, which people will be able to refer to over and over, often after difficult phone calls and experiences. It's a psychological boost, evidence of your people's great value and ability.

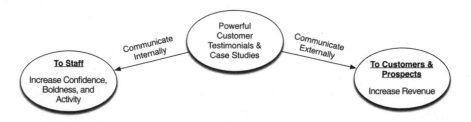

**Figure 19.1   The Two Directional Power of Customer Testimonials**

**Create a central repository of testimonials.** Create a company spreadsheet or slide deck with every testimonial you have listed there. Allow people easy access so that they can get to, enjoy, and utilize these powerful, positive statements for revenue growth. This is the place people will go to when it's time to communicate your testimonials to the outside world, which is the focus of the rest of this chapter.

## Rule of Thumb: Everything that Leaves Your Office Should Contain a Testimonial

Every communication that leaves your office is made stronger by a testimonial.

Which means, basically, that everything that customers and prospects see should contain a testimonial.

Testimonials make your materials stronger, more interesting, more compelling, truer, bolder, more resonant, more connecting, and flat-out better. So, put them everywhere. Every page of every thing.

There is no wrong place for a testimonial.

Here are some of the many ways you can communicate yours.

*Testimonial Guidelines*
1. Use names, job titles, and company names. If you don't, I'm wondering what you're hiding. Or maybe you made the testimonial up? Your customer has given you permission to use her comments in your materials. Do so.
2. In general, one to three sentences is a good length for a testimonial. But there is no wrong length. If you're communicating them and yours are a half-page long, I won't argue.
3. The testimonial could be any testimonial, it doesn't matter. Don't spend too much time deciding which testimonial to communicate. Pick one, copy, paste, go.
4. When communicating testimonials directly to people (that's what I call active testimonial communication, see the next section), target your existing testimonials to peers. This is important. We want owners to hear about your owner customers and purchasing managers to hear from fellow buyers. We *do not* want to direct compliments from purchasing to owners of other firms. It won't resonate. Different things are important to them.

## Where to Communicate Testimonials

There are active and passive ways to communicate testimonials. Active communication means you're doing it personally, and the recipient is reading or hearing the testimonials directly from you. In this case, the testimonials are the point of the communication. Passive testimonial communication occurs when you add testimonials to other content, like your website, catalog, or invoices. In this case, the testimonial serves to enhance and improve the impact of the material it's added to.

### *Active Testimonial Communication*

Active testimonial communications are among the most powerful revenue-generating actions you can engage in. Basically, you're delivering the happy words of your customers to other customers and prospects. You can do so by email or verbally.

These are one-on-one techniques.

Let's take a look at both approaches.

### *Direct Emails to Customers and Prospects*

In terms of growing your business, the very best thing you can do with a testimonial is to email it to a customer or prospect and suggest delivering the same kind of value to the person you're writing to. These emails are brief, really fast to write—it's all about the copy and paste—and have generated a great deal of revenue for my clients.

Here is an example of one such email. Use it as is or adjust it to use language you are comfortable with. Note that the testimonial used is from the previous chapter and actually combines two separate testimonials into one.

Chris,

I hope you're well.

I was thinking about you the other day, and I realized we have a customer similar to you. He happens to be one of our fastest-growing customers, and this is what he told us recently about our work:

Working with X Co. accounts for 23% of our annual revenue growth! I think that's pretty awesome, don't you? X Co. Is a definitely a partner to us. A vendor just sells your product. But a partner cares about you. A partner is interested in your profitable growth and does what he can to help you attain that growth. That's what X Co. does for us.

—Tom Johnson, owner and CEO, Amazing Contractors, Inc.

Like you, Tom runs his company, which is about the size of your firm. Why don't we talk about applying the same kind of value to your company? I'd be happy to tell you exactly what we do for Tom, as I think it would be of enormous help to you and your customers, too.
What's better for you, Wednesday afternoon or Thursday morning?

Best regards,
Joe

Three notes:

1. **Aspiration plays a big role.** We want prospects to desire the benefits and value that your successful customers enjoy. If I'm the owner who's receiving this email, I want 23% revenue growth too!
2. **Give date and time options for speaking.** This goes for all of your sales communication: Don't ask them if they'd like to speak, assume they do. Then give two specific options so that they can select one. This way, they have more yes options than no options. My business mentor, Alan Weiss, calls this "a choice of yesses," which is always better than a choice between yes and no.
3. **Follow up once or twice after sending.** These days, so many emails get picked off by spam filters. This offers us a terrific reason to follow up. A lot of business is lost because of a lack of follow-up. So, if you don't hear from this prospect, send another email in a day or two to make sure the testimonial arrived. And a phone call a week after sending the email would be a good idea as well.

## Communicating Testimonials in Conversation

The other highly effective way to actively communicate testimonials is in conversation. Here, it's okay to paraphrase the testimonial. You can:

- Make a call specifically to communicate a testimonial.
- Add it on to an existing conversation. "By the way, I meant to tell you, we have a customer . . ."

- Leave it in a voice mail. This is the least impactful of the three, but, as with every technique in the book, it's better than not communicating at all.

Here's what verbally communicating a testimonial sounds like:

"Listen, Chris, I was thinking about you the other day, and I realized we have a customer similar to you. Like you, he's the owner. Contracting company. About the same size as yours. We talked recently, and he told me working with us accounts for 23% of his revenue growth! Can you believe that? I couldn't believe it. Why don't I tell you about what he buys from us? I'd love to discuss applying the same kind value to your company. Do you have a few minutes now or should we connect on Thursday morning?"

The key here is that it's perfectly okay to put the customer's testimonial in to your own words.

Further, when sharing a testimonial verbally, you may choose to identify the customer or not, your call. Sometimes in conversation it can be awkward to use a name, title, and company. This is the only place it's okay to exclude a name and company. It's the only exception. Everywhere else, the testimonial is written, and it demands a name, job title, and company.

### Passive Testimonial Communication

Think of the list below as vehicles for your testimonials.

Testimonials improve each of the items below and also allow for customers and prospects to imagine working with you and buying more and different products.

These are company-to-many techniques.

Unless otherwise noted, all of these testimonials should include the customers' names, job titles, and companies.

**Your website.** Every page should have a testimonial. Every product page. Every service page. Every time somebody clicks a link on your Web site they should see a testimonial. But don't worry about adding them to every page immediately. Just update one page at a time. Small improvements add up to big revenue growth. And you can repeat testimonials. If you have a large website with hundreds of pages, it's okay for the same testimonial to appear on three of them. No issues with this at all.

**Your newsletter.** A good newsletter goes out every two weeks and has a dedicated space for a testimonial. Just paste it in. Newsletter structure is detailed in Chapter 30.

**Email signatures.** A lot of my clients have had success using testimonials in their email signature, with the testimonial appearing *above* the signature, so it does not look like it's part of the signature. Rotate these weekly. If you can set up and edit signatures companywide, that would be ideal. This way, you'll know every person receiving email from your company is seeing the powerfully positive words of your customers.

**Proposals/quotes/contracts.** One of the best times for customers or prospects to see a testimonial is when they are making their decision to buy. And one of the best ways to increase the likelihood of them buying more is to include testimonials on your proposals, quotes, or contracts. Whatever you use to sign up business, paste testimonials there. You want to be careful to use the testimonials of peers. Show customers and prospects how dramatically their peers have improved—in their own words—when they've made a similar purchase from you. It's strong stuff!

**Invoices.** Want to collect faster and more? Add testimonials to your invoices. Rotate frequently.

**Your catalog and collateral.** All collateral is improved with testimonials. Further, if you have a catalog or a marketing folder, every page can use a testimonial. Here, too, it's okay to repeat. Next time you go to print, ask an administrative person at your office to add a testimonial to every page of whatever is being printed.

**Your lobby or entry area.** Many companies have a monitor in their reception area. Run a slide show of testimonials there. People's eyes wander as they wait. Let them read what people love about doing business with you. Only good things can result.

**Your on-hold message.** Some people play annoying music. Why not play testimonials? You can either summarize them yourself ("Our customers tell us . . .") or play snippets of your audio recording. In this case, you'll want to get additional permission from your customers.

**Chapter Summary**

- Communicate testimonials *everywhere*. Target them peer-to-peer. Owners should hear from other owners, engineers from engineers.
- You can communicate testimonials one-on-one, by email, or verbally on the phone or face-to-face.
- Similarly, testimonials should be placed throughout your existing marketing materials—like your website, catalog, and other print materials—and in your newsletter, proposals, or quotes, and anything else customers and prospects look at.
- There's probably no wrong place for a testimonial!

# 20 | Growth Technique #3: Create Short, Powerful Case Studies

Good case studies describe *what* your customer bought, *why he* bought it, and how he was improved by doing business with you. That's it.

Good case studies are short. In fact, they should never be longer than one page. Why ask people to read all of those details? Just tell your readers about how you helped your customer.

## A Case Study Comes from Customer Interviews

If you interviewed your customer to collect testimonials, you have everything you need to create an effective case study. Same conversation. *You don't have to talk with them again.* One interaction of 5 to 10 minutes gets you everything you need for numerous testimonials and a case study.

## The Four Parts of a Good Study

A good case study has four parts:

1. *The problem.* What was wrong when the customer came to you? Why did the customer come to you? What problem did she need to solve? This is one or two sentences.
2. *The solution.* What did they buy? Name your product, service, or project here. This is one or two sentences.
3. *The value.*
   - This is your longest section.
   - It is made up of bullet points.
   - Describe how your customer improved as a result of buying your product.
   - What got better?
   - Did the business grow? Did the customer save time? Did the customer make her customers happy?
   - Detail the qualitative, quantitative, and emotional value your customer expressed.
   - These should be in the third person.
4. *A testimonial.* Paste in a testimonial from this customer's collection.

Give your testimonial a good title. Think of it as a newspaper headline, but as with all of this work, don't overthink it. Just write it and move.

Include a photo. Place yours where you like, but I put mine in the upper right. The photos I use are almost always a headshot or professional photo of my client. When that's not possible, I use their company logo. Or a shot of their building. Or, if it's well known, an image of their product. Least desirable is an image of the product you sold them.

## Sample Case Study

Here's a case study, based on the interview with Tom Johnson I transcribed in Chapter 18. My comments are in italics.

## X Co. Helps Amazing Contractors, Inc. Grow by 23%

| |
|---|
| A headshot of the customer would go here. |

### Customer

Tom Johnson, CEO and owner, Amazing Contractors, Inc. (I made this company name up; any real company by this name is pure coincidence!)

## The Problem

Customer was experiencing late shipments from his past supplier, and, as a result, his skilled laborers were standing around without product. This became too expensive in a hurry.

*Note: What contractor hasn't experienced this? This case study immediately resonates with other general contractors who are reading it. And it's general contractors that this case study will be communicated to.*

## The Solution

The customer started buying equipment from us. It started with lumber, then doorframes, and then it expanded to flooring and roofing.

*Note: Just list the products this customer buys. If there are product numbers, include them here, along with very brief descriptions of the items. Use bullet points if you think it'll help.*

## The Value

- The customer reported that out of 50 total suppliers he uses, X Co. ranks #1.
- We're proud to report that the customer also states that working with us accounts for 23% of his annual revenue growth! "I think that's pretty awesome, don't you?" said our customer, Tom Johnson.
- Customer states he views us as a partner, not a vendor. He says we care about him, his firm, and his profitable growth.
- The customer says X Co. helps his firm solve issues for his customers that others simply aren't able to solve. This helps grow his business.
- Customer reports we help him make his customers look good. We're thrilled about this!

*Note: This section simply reports what the customer told you, but in your own words. It's also helpful to mix your own comments and personality into these items. For example, I added language about being proud and thrilled about these results.*

### Customer Testimonial

X Co. really innovates. They're always adding new products. Several times they've actually introduced new ideas to us that we hadn't even thought about. As a result, X Co. helps us get the sale and helps us solve issues for our customers that somebody else isn't even able to solve. X Co. helps to grow our business. They help us handle more work and help us make our customers look really good.

—Tom Johnson, owner and CEO,
Top New England General Contracting

*Note: Longer testimonials are acceptable within case studies, as they support and enhance the value items that are in your words.*

That's it.

One page.

This should take you no more than 15 minutes to write, because the notes are already written from your interview.

Save it as a PDF.

Share its location with everyone in your firm.

Ask them to send it to other owners and CEOs in a similar role. Complete details on communicating case studies are included in the next chapter.

---

### Chapter Summary

- A good case study is one page long, and takes about 15 minutes to write.
- The content of the case study is based on the testimonial interview you've already done.
- There are four parts: the problem, the solution (what you sold), the value experienced by the customer, and a testimonial from this customer.

# 21

# Growth Technique #4: Communicate Case Studies to People Who Can Buy from You

Like testimonials, case studies need to be communicated to people who can buy from us.

And like testimonials, case studies should be targeted to peers of the people being profiled. You can categorize your case studies by job title, industry or vertical, and company size, for example. Choose the categories that make sense to you.

And like testimonials, they can be communicated by your management, salespeople, and customer service people one-on-one to customers and prospects; and they can be delivered to groups of people via company-to-many marketing.

Here are some ways you can communicate these powerful descriptions of your great value.

## By Email, One-On-One

The most effective way to deliver your testimonials is by private email, directly to a customer or prospect. Here's what it should look like:

Joe:

   I noticed we're working with a company similar to yours. Attached, please find a case study that details the great value the customer has experienced. I'm certain we can deliver the same value to your organization. In fact, I think you use the products this customer purchased from us—only you don't buy them from us. Can we connect briefly about this on Monday morning or Wednesday afternoon? What's better for you?

   Best regards,

   Christine


   Attach testimonial.

   Send.

   Total time invested: about 45 seconds.


## By Email, to Your List

This is the same idea, but slightly less personal and a far wider reach.

   Let's say you have a case study written up about a purchasing agent in a $50 million distributor. You would go to your list (details on building a good list are in Chapter 28), and select all of the purchasing agents of companies that are approximately in this revenue range. Maybe there are 35 of them on your list, some customers, some prospects. Start an email to them that goes something like this:

   I'm writing because I noticed we were working with a highly effective head of purchasing, much like yourself. She has told us recently about the wonderful value our firm has delivered to her. This is detailed in the attached case study. I thought you might be interested in reading through her experiences, and perhaps discussing applying the same kind of value to your organization. Further, I'm eager to hear your feedback on this. What's good for you, Thursday at 9 a.m. or 2 p.m.?

   Look forward to connecting!

   Best regards,

   Allan


   It's slightly less personal than the one-on-one approach, but it's highly effective because so many people are receiving it.

Attach case study.

Send.

Total time invested: 3 minutes (including searching your database to quickly select peer recipients).

## By Postal Mail

Case studies make for excellent mailings. To really get it noticed, use FedEx.

Select a peer of the person that's written up.

Print testimonial on nice paper.

Add a handwritten note, perhaps on the case study itself. Ask for a conversation to get the recipient's feedback.

Address envelope.

Send.

Total time investment: 5 to 10 minutes.

## Create a Powerful Book of Case Studies

Have a graphic designer lay out an incredibly effective book of case studies. It should feature a sexy cover and a letter from the president, CEO, or owner.

Include one case study per page, and you can use large photography on facing pages, to show the person being profiled, the company buildings, logos, or the products the company makes. You can even add the product or service the company buys from you.

Have these professionally printed and bound in magazine form, or whatever structure moves you.

Send to customers and prospects, and distribute to your staff internally. All new hires should receive one on their first day with you. It's a really effective marketing piece that clearly details your value in the words of your customers.

These are the top four ways to communicate testimonials, but I'm sure you can think of your own and add them to the list. Remember, there's no wrong way to do this. Get creative. Think of communication pathways you're good at and that you will enjoy. Then try them! See what happens. Make it an adventure!

**Chapter Summary**

- Communicate your case studies internally to staff and externally to customers and prospects.
- The best way to get testimonials in front of customers and prospects is by direct, personal email.
- You can also email groups of people from your list—this is slightly less personal but offers a far wider reach.
- Consider the postal service or FedEx to get your case studies into the hands of people who can buy from you.
- And finally, a professionally designed book of case studies is a tremendous way to impress customers and prospects and encourage them to do more business with you.

# 22

# Growth Technique #5: The Million-Dollar Question— This One Technique Can Grow Your Business by 10% Immediately

They are your best customers or your average ones.

They've been with you for months, or years, or decades.

You've shown them catalogs, sent them promotions, and detailed your products and services countless times. You've been to their offices, and they've been to yours. Perhaps you've golfed together, lunched together, and had drinks together.

They *must* know about everything they can buy from you, right?

Sadly, no, they don't.

Just as you are, your customers are busy. They have their own issues, problems, and emergencies throughout the day. They have their own fires, bosses, and families to think about. They worry about their own businesses, just as you worry about yours. They don't have time to think about your product catalog or service range. Simply, your customers are unaware of everything they can buy from you.

*And people cannot buy what they are not aware of.*

So, we must make them aware.

## Ask Yourself This Simple Question

Think about your entire catalog of products, services, and offerings—everything that a customer can buy from you, from start to finish. Got it? *What percentage of all this is your average customer aware of?*

Before continuing to read, really think about this and arrive at a number. It's a really important figure, so give it 30 seconds of consideration. When you have it, write it down in the margin here.

I've asked this question hundreds of times to tens of thousands of people. On stage at speeches and in conference rooms at clients' offices. I've asked during webinars and in workshop rooms. I call this number your *awareness percentage*. Do you know what the average awareness percentage is?

Twenty-five percent.

Across industries, from manufacturing companies to distributors, from service providers to retailers, business leaders tell me that on average, their customers do not know about three-quarters of what they sell. Think about the gravity of this.

You dramatically improve your customers' lives and companies, right? You've done the hard work of converting them from prospects to customers, and many of them have become repeat customers. Your salespeople call on them, meet with them, and have trusting, respectful relationships with them. These customers enjoy and appreciate your work, because they keep coming back to you. They are being called on by competitors regularly, but they stay with you. Daily, weekly, monthly, as they decline to do business with your competition, they decide again and again to keep working with *you*. You have them. You've earned them. They're happy.

And yet, they only know about a tiny fraction of what you do. They cannot possibly benefit from the rest of your offerings, because they simply have no awareness of them. You haven't systematically communicated everything else that your existing customers can buy from you.

*You* know everything your customers can buy from you because you think about your offerings daily. But your customers spend their days dealing with their own issues and offerings, not yours.

How many times have you heard something like this from your good customers?

*"Wait, you mean you do that too?"*

Or, *"I didn't know you sell that!"*

They need it. You can sell it to them and help them tremendously. You assume they know this. But they don't. It's almost tragic.

## A Slight Increase in Awareness Catapults Sales

We don't need to aim for 100% awareness. That's probably impossible—even Apple's customers don't have active awareness of everything the company puts out, from hardware to software to services.

In fact, with my clients, I've discovered that even a small increase, say 10% or 15%, will move sales dramatically. Actually, sales growth often exceeds the awareness increase. This means that if you succeed at raising awareness by 10%, sales can grow 15% to 23%. Aim for improvement, not perfection. Improvement is enough to generate a lot of new revenue for you.

## How to Increase Your Awareness Percentage

Increasing your awareness percentage is extraordinarily easy. It's so straightforward that you're going to shake your head. And you're going to ask yourself—correctly— *"Why haven't I been doing this?"* How much money has this cost you? How much will it cost you if you don't apply this technique from this day forth?

During every interaction with your existing customers, ask this million-dollar question:

*Did you know we also do X?* (X is simply the new product or service you're promoting to this customer.)

Ask every customer you talk to—on the phone or in person—giving them an easy opportunity to buy more from you every time you interact with them. We don't ask as a salesperson trying to sell. We ask as a colleague, a trusted partner, trying to help.

### For a Printer

"Really quick, while I have you, did you know that in addition to printing your marketing pieces we can mail them for you, so you never have to see or touch them? Most people aren't aware we do this, and I wanted to make sure you knew."

### For an Attorney

"Thanks for your trust in having us handle your case. Did you know we also handle intellectual property issues? If you have two minutes now, I'd be happy to discuss it with you, or we can schedule something for Thursday if that's more convenient."

### For a Manufacturer

"We're grateful for your business, and we love being able to make these parts for you. Did you know we also make these other components as well? I've noticed a lot of my customers in your area have been buying them, and I wanted to make sure you knew."

When you ask the "did you know" question, your customers are not turned off or repelled somehow. To the contrary, they're pleased to learn about another opportunity to benefit from your tremendous value. People prefer to buy multiple products or services from partners they like working with. Why would you withhold this additional value from them?

## How to Ask the "Did You Know" Question

The best way to ask the "did you know" question is one-on-one—on the phone or in person. This is yet another technique that requires your personal involvement. An email is not enough here. (An email is better than nothing but markedly less effective than asking customers within a conversation.) When we ask personally, we can gauge the reaction, assess the customer's tone, and decide on the best path forward. The customer is able to ask us questions or express an interest. We are able to dig a bit if we wish and ask a follow-up question if necessary. An email lets us accomplish none of this. In this case—and in almost all cases—the phone call and the personal conversation generate far better results than the email.

## As an Add-On to an Existing Conversation

Specifically, the best "did you know" questions are added on to the end of an existing conversation. Say a customer calls in with a concern or issue. You resolve it for them, and at the end of the conversation, you say something like this:

*Have I resolved your issue? Thank you for giving me the opportunity to make it right. I appreciate that. We love working with you on this. By the way, did you know we also provide this other service?*

This can happen on a sales call, a customer service conversation, or any conversation at all.

(Among my clients, a lot of new revenue results from sentences that begin with "By the way . . .". You can accomplish a lot of great things using well-planned "by the way" statements.)

## As a Stand-Alone Call

It's also perfectly reasonable to call customers specifically to increase their awareness about your offerings. You begin the conversation, as with every interaction, with a focus on your customer's well-being and self-interest:

> Just giving you a quick call to make sure you're pleased with our work and that we're serving you well. Is everything going according to plan? Are we meeting your expectations? I'm so glad to hear that. Please don't hesitate to reach out to me directly if you ever have a concern or an area you need us to improve. We really value your trust. By the way, I noticed you were buying a lot of X from us, but not taking advantage of Y. Did you know we also do Y? I'd be happy to discuss it with you now, or we can schedule something for Tuesday if you'd prefer.

You call with a genuine interest in how you're doing for your customer. And you close the conversation by planting a quick seed about another product you can help this person with.

## Who Should Ask?

Every customer-facing staff member in your organization can and should be asking this question.

> **Executives:** Nothing bad ever happens when a corporate leader informs his or her high-level peer at the customer's organization about another way you can add value.
>
> **Salespeople:** Make the call. Take the order. Thank them for their business. Then ask the did you know question.
>
> **Customer service professionals:** Perhaps more than any other department in your company, customer service has a golden opportunity to systematically ask the did you know question. Customer service has two primary purposes: To take repeat orders and resolve concerns. Either way, they are dealing with existing customers all day long. Who better to ask this simple question?

## Strategies for Systematizing the Did You Know Question

The system is the key here. One-off efforts won't generate the critical mass required to significantly affect your awareness percentage, and in turn, your revenue. Ideally, multiple people with varying customer-facing responsibilities, are asking this question multiple times a day at the end of existing conversations. Ideally, if you have a customer service department, they're asking this question to everyone they talk to.

### *Strategically, One-on-One*

One way to ask the did you know question is to quickly look over a customer's order history with your company, and simply promote a product or service that complements what they're currently buying. This is a one-at-a-time approach, which requires that you strategically choose a product or service you think would resonate with each customer. You'd spend 30 seconds picking the product or service and another 30 seconds actually asking the question. This approach is best suited for smaller or solo-practitioner firms.

## *Rotate Focus as a Company*

Another way of doing this is to select a product or service for everyone in the company to focus on for a period of time. Usually two to four weeks is an ideal amount of time. During this period, everybody is asking the did you know question about the same product or service. You're making a concerted push to raise the awareness about one specific product or service. Once the time period expires, you move on to the next product or service. The larger a company is, the better this approach works.

## *Track Who Gets Asked, as Simply as Possible*

As simply as possible, track who gets asked the did you know question and what about. If you use a companywide CRM platform, that's probably the best place for this kind of tracking. Otherwise, the simplest tracking tool in my experience is a spreadsheet. Create one for your company for use by all customer-facing people asking this question. It should have the following columns:

- Employee Name
- Date of Did You Know Question
- Customer Name
- Company
- Product or Service Promoted

That's it. Nothing else is necessary.

We want to track our progress this way because we want to carefully detail who we ask and what we ask them about. We do not want customers hearing about the same product repeatedly over the course of a week. This allows us to keep track of things. Ideally, you want to ask the did you know question no more than every two to three weeks.

## *The "Did You Know" Sticky Note*

I like simple solutions, because they are almost always the best solutions. The key to increasing sales quickly with the technique in this chapter is *remembering to ask.* We want a number of people asking the "did you know" question throughout the day. Too often we get caught up in the urgent issues of the day and end up reacting our way through the day. Blink, and the day is gone.

So, how do we remind ourselves to ask the did you know question? Try the highly technical and complex yellow sticky note. In large capital letters, write down "DYK?" on a sticky note, and place it onto the bottom of your computer monitor. If you make phone calls while driving, stick it onto your dashboard.

If you have another way to remind yourself to ask this revenue-generating question, do it. It doesn't matter how you remember to ask—only that you ask, regularly and systematically.

You deserve the extra revenue.

And your customers deserve to benefit from even more of your value.

---

## Chapter Summary

- Your average customer is aware of only a small percentage of what they can buy from you.
- It's your job to increase this awareness percentage among your customers.
- Ask the did you know question about products and services you want to promote.
- All customer-facing people should ask this question systematically, at the end of every phone call. Additionally, executives and salespeople can call customers for the express purpose of asking this question.

# 23 | Growth Technique #6: How to Get Referrals

There are few better ways to grow your business than referrals, yet we hesitate.

There are few more effective ways to expand your prospect list, bring on new customers, and grow your business. Yet, the vast majority of small and mid-size owners, executives, managers, salespeople, and customer service people quickly—if sadly—admit that they do not ask enough.

There are various reasons for this, mostly our own discomfort, which we covered in Chapter 12. The happy customer tends to be not only agreeable but actually excited to send us her contacts. That's because she knows we'll serve them well, they'll be taken care of, and it will not only make her friend or colleague happy, but it will make her, the referrer, look good.

Another reason that people often give for not asking for referrals more is they don't really know what to do. They don't know how.

This chapter will change that.

This chapter covers three ways to ask for referrals. They include two easy, fast techniques and one that's a bit more involved but highly successful. As always, pay attention to the language, which is the key to not only obtaining referrals but quite probably the entire revenue growth process.

Remember, you help people tremendously. Do you believe people in your target market are better off working with you than with your competition? If so, go and get them!

We begin with a general rule of thumb.

## Don't Use the Word "Referral"

Get used to asking for referrals without using the word, because as soon as you say "referral," people get strange. They clam up. They feel pressure to come up with a name, on the spot, which screws up what is otherwise an easy, painless process. So, don't use the word referral when you're asking for one.

## Request Referrals by Phone or in Person

Have you ever asked for a referral by email? If so, did you get the referral? Nearly 100% of emailed referral requests go without a response. Silence is the answer to the emailed referral request. Because your customers are busy. They have their own fires. And here you come with an email asking them to do work on your behalf (that's how they perceive it), and they'd rather not tell you "no." So they tell you nothing.

The referral techniques in this chapter should be used in conversation, on the phone or in person. Deal with it on the spot, and move on. No sense in waiting around your inbox for an email that's not coming.

## Referral Technique #1: Connection to Another Company

"Who else do you know like yourself—an owner/admin/purchasing agent—at another company who would get similar value from working with us?"

This is a broad request in which you're asking for anybody else your customer may know. Perfectly reasonable, and entirely possibly somebody obvious will pop into their minds.

Note the language "like yourself," indicating we want someone in a similar position. Feel free to spell it out for your customers, identify the job title or job titles you're looking for.

Also, the focus is on "similar value," not customers, or sales, or revenue. Who else would appreciate a "similar value" as you do? Who else would benefit from working with us like you do? Who else would enjoy working with us like you do? For who else would we save time and grow revenue like we do for you?

"What customers or vendors do you work with who would find value in working with us?"

This question narrows it down for your customer, asking her to think about her other vendors, or her customers specifically.

"I know you work with Z Company. Who do you work with there who would find value in doing business with us?"

Ask for a contact at as specific company. If you're targeting doing business with a certain firm, think through your list of happy customers and try to anticipate who might know somebody there. Then ask for a connection.

## Referral Technique #2: Internal Connection

"We love working with you, Mike. Who else at your firm is in your position who would get value from working with us?"

Here, you're asking for your customer's colleagues inside the business. What other general managers are there? Or purchasing managers in another department?

"Mike, you're one of our best customers. Is there somebody in the X division in your position who we should be talking to?"

Name the division of the company you want to be referred into. This works best for larger companies where you've had success with one unit and wish to expand your business.

## Referral Technique #3: Plant the Seed, Harvest the Fruit

This approach takes a bit longer, but it results in referrals in a great percentage of the instances you implement it. In fact, if you follow my suggestions here, this technique generates referrals two out of three times you apply. (Pretty good compared to the referral return rate on email requests, right?)

*Step 1: Plant the Seed (but Do Not Ask) for a Referral*

When an order comes in, thank the prospect for his business, and then say the following:

"A few days after the order arrives [or a few days into or after the project] I will give you a call personally to make sure we've served you well. At that time, assuming you're happy and everything went well, I will ask you for your recommendation regarding somebody like you who would also get value from working with us. Sound okay?"

In all my years of asking this question, and of my clients asking this question, I have not experienced a single "no." Everybody agrees. They agree because it's an easy yes. Who would argue with you following up to make sure everything went well? And if it does, why *wouldn't* they refer you?

Think about what's happening here.

You're not asking for a referral.

You are *promising* to ask for a referral. That's different.

And, critically, the customer is promising to give you one.

It's mutual accountability to the referral: you will put it on your calendar to ask when you promise. And the customer promises to have somebody for you when you ask. It's beautiful referral choreography!

*Step 2: Harvest Your Referral*

When the appointed date and time comes, make your call.

"How did we do? Did everything arrive on time? Did we serve you well?"

If the answer yes, continue with this:

"That's great to hear. We value your business very much. When we talked last, you kindly agreed to connect me with someone like you who'd also get value from working with us. Who did you come up with?"

And . . . stop.

Don't say another word.

Wait for your customer to say something.

There's a lot of business value in silence.

At this point, about one-third of your customers—the people who actually thought through a connection for you in the days since you last spoke—will have a referral for you. Thirty-three percent. That's 33% more referrals than you would get from asking by email!

Two-thirds will have an excuse. They'll say something about not being able to think of anyone. Or, they don't think they know anyone who would make sense. Or they'll keep thinking about it. (Right, sure they will!)

Now, you have my permission to put them on the spot. They made you a promise. You made a promise, too, but you're keeping your promise. They're not keeping theirs. So, help your customer out and describe the kinds of people you usually work with.

"We typically work with project managers like yourself, but also general managers and heads of purchasing. Do you know anyone like that at your firm or perhaps at a vendor of yours?"

Again, say it and stop. Listen for the answer. Breathe.

At this point, another one-third of these customers will magically think of a referral.

That's a two-thirds referral return rate. Pretty good right?

Everyone else will struggle and say they still can't think of someone. At this point, you can let them off the hook and thank them for trying.

## What to Do When Somebody Gives You a Referral

This section sounds self-explanatory, but this point is important.

Ask your customer if they'd like to make the introduction or if they'd prefer you simply use their name. Make your preference clear: "I'd love it if you could introduce us."

An introduction is better, but the name-dropping is certainly much better than reaching out to the prospect cold.

Get clear on what your customer prefers, and ask for the introduction.

## Finally, Call the Referral ASAP

Too many people wait around before calling their referral.

I've learned the hard way in my career that time is no friend of deals—or referrals!

If somebody recommends a good prospective customer to you, call that person within 24 hours. Make that your rule of thumb; reach out within one business day.

In revenue growth, procrastination costs money.

---

**Chapter Summary**

- Don't use the word "referral" when asking for them.
- You can ask for referrals by job title. Ask to be referred to somebody else within the same company or at another specific firm.
- Use the plant-and-harvest referral method: *promise* to ask for a referral at a specific date and time when your customer places the order. Then, when the time comes, ask for the referral!
- Don't forget to request the introduction, and then call your referral within one business day to introduce yourself and start talking business.

# 24 | Growth Technique #7: The Power of Owner Calls

Here's a simple but really powerful communication technique, which nearly all of my clients implement. Universally and unanimously, they love this approach. Everyone who tries this tells me of its power and incredible effectiveness. Like nearly every other technique in this book, it's smart but incredibly simple.

If you're the owner, president, or CEO, pick up the phone and call a customer. Say something like this, in language that's comfortable for you:

> "Sally, this is Angela Thomas, one of the owners here at XYZ Corp. Listen, I just wanted to check in with you and make sure we're serving you well. Is everything going great? You're pleased with our work? Is there anything I can do for you? Please don't ever hesitate to reach out to me directly if I can add value for you."

If your customer doesn't pick up, leave a voice message with basically the exact same language. A voice mail with this message has equal power to an actual conversation, but demands just a fraction of the time. I tell my clients to *hope* the voice mail picks up!

If you're a manager or an executive at your firm, make the same call, using the same language. Add something like this: "I know you usually deal with Anne, who's wonderful. She reports to me and speaks so highly of you. I wanted to call you personally to thank you for your business and to make sure we're serving you well."

Remember toward the beginning of this book, I told you that revenue growth is proactive work? This technique is the definition of proactive action. You are the only owner or manager that your customers work with who will be making these calls.

Actually having these conversations, by the way, is a pleasure. The customer is thrilled to hear from you and delighted to speak with you.

The power of this simple act is extraordinary.

It deepens relationships and cements trust, which almost always leads to additional business in the near term.

---

**Chapter Summary**

As an owner, executive, or manager, make proactive phone calls to customers, inquire as to their happiness, and make yourself available for direct contact. You'll be the only one doing so; the competition certainly is not making these calls.

# 25 | Growth Technique #8: The Seven-Figure Follow-Up Process

Do you send out a lot of quotes, or estimates?

Or maybe your business, like mine, uses proposals to frame projects and fees?

Many of my clients have sizable teams that take phone calls for new estimates all day long. Some companies call this group customer service, and others call it inside sales.

I was recently doing a series of workshops for a client as a part of our year-long revenue growth project together.

This company had about 80 people in customer service.

Each person generated between 20 and 50 quotes a day. About 23% of them close and turn into business.

That means almost 80% evaporate into the wind.

I asked them how many of those are followed up upon?

Answer: almost none.

Can't blame them. They're busy. Their phones are ringing off the hook. They have so many demands for so much reactive work, where would they find time to follow up?

Here's the thing: These quotes are existing customers asking to do more business with you.

If you send them a price and they never hear from you again, the odds are they've given their business to somebody else—who did follow up.

Let's do some math related to the quotes my client's customer service department generates.

Let's say 80 people generate 20 quotes a day (I like to use the most conservative number in these kinds of discussions).

That's 1,600 quotes a day, which is 8,000 quotes per week, which is 6,000 quotes per month.

Which is 400,000 quotes per year.

Twenty percent close, that's 80,000.

That leaves 320,000 quotes that are not closed. And these customers hardly ever heard from my client again. (That changed in a hurry, by the way. Like, the next day.)

So now let's imagine a simple quote follow-up process that consists of three emails following the sending of the quote.

Email one goes out a week after the initial quote and says something like this:

> "I wanted to make sure you received my quote, as these things tend to get picked off by spam filters. Please confirm if you go it, and where we stand with your order."

If you get a reply, stop the follow-up process and respond accordingly.

If you don't hear anything, send email two, which should say something like:

> "I hope you're well. We got an order for the same products you asked me to quote two weeks ago, and I thought of you. Should we plan for your order or have you gone in another direction?"

And if you don't hear back after this one, send one, final email, no more than three weeks after the initial quote went out. Also, feel free to adjust the time frames to your business structure. You may need to send them closer to the quote, or much more spaced out, depending on how much time typically passes between a quote or a proposal and an order in your business.

Email three should include this line. "Thanks for the opportunity to quote you X, Y, and Z. Since I haven't heard from you, I'll be closing our file on this order. If you decide to purchase, please let me know within 24 hours."

You have every right, and even every duty, to be this bold.

Remember how much you help people. If you forget how much you help your customers, just ask them. They'll tell you.

You can send these emails yourself. Or you can assign an administrative assistant to follow up on quotes.

And if you want to get even more proactive, replace the last email with a phone call.

Two emails and a phone call. That should get you to a yes or a no. And if the customer still doesn't reply, he's simply being rude and unprofessional. He asked you for a quote, you delivered, and he refused to give you an answer.

Back to some simple mathematics.

Let's say that even though these are your existing customers, and you know they need this stuff because they've asked you to bid on it, you only close 2% of the quotes you follow up on. (It'll likely be closer to 10%, but again, let's be conservative.)

That, my friend, is 6,400 additional sales per year.

Let's assume an average order size of $1,100.

For my client, that's an extra $7 million. (And if they closed 10% of their follow-ups instead of the ridiculously low 2% we're using, this number becomes $35 million.)

What would the number be for you?

Work through *your* numbers now. It only takes a minute, and it's a fun process. It should also move you to action.

There's millions of dollars in quote and proposal follow-up.

Will you do it?

---

## Chapter Summary

- Quote follow-up is one of the communication activities that generates the most revenue with the least amount of work.
- Consider the vast number of quotes that you send out, which are never—or only lightly—followed up upon.
- Think about a three-communication follow-up process: email/email/email, or email/email/call.

# 26 | Growth Technique #9: The Magic of the Handwritten Note

A number of years ago, I received a handwritten note from a woman who attended one of my association speeches. It was written on a full-size sheet of paper. In the note, she described the impact my presentation had on her business and her life. She talked about how she changed her mindset and started marketing daily. She felt more successful, and her bank accounts confirmed this.

As soon as I read this note, I was finished with it. Sure, it made me feel wonderful. It was extremely thoughtful of her to write it. And I was thrilled with her success, as I am with everyone who reports their progress to me. But it took me exactly one minute to read this note, and then I had no more purpose for the sheet of paper it was written on.

And yet, years later, the note is still on my credenza. And I keep a clean workspace. At the end of every day, my desk is clean. I like to see the top of my desk, and piles make me anxious. But this handwritten note, the only one I've received not counting holiday cards, has a rather permanent place in my office.

We've even moved since I first received this note. I've also remodeled my office in the years since it arrived. Yet, this piece of paper still has a prominent place in my workspace. I cannot bring myself to throw it away.

Why?

First, because the woman who sent it cared enough to take the time to do so. That's meaningful and important.

And even more important, because it reminds me to write my own handwritten notes regularly.

## Why Send Handwritten Notes

I recently traveled to Texas to meet with a prospect—a manufacturer of industrial parts. The owner was at the meeting, as was his general manager and his head of sales. We were discussing a relatively large project to help grow this company's annual revenue. We had a nice meeting. But a few days later, when I spoke with the owner and the general manager, they told me that the sales manager was hesitating for various reasons.

After getting a good grasp of the reasons for resistance, I hung up the phone and took out one of my Montana fountain pens. On nice, thick, good-looking paper, I wrote to the owner, addressing the salesperson's concerns. (When you have to make a choice of whom to address, always deal with the highest-level buyer possible; if the owner is on board, no resistance from the sales manager can overcome it.) A few days later, the owner called and said we're on, let's roll. Did the note get me the business? Not by itself, but I'm certain my competition didn't send a note to the owner, nor did the sales manager! Not coincidentally, the sales manager parted ways with the company not long after this exchange, and my client went on to enjoy significant revenue growth in the years ahead.

**You should send handwritten notes because they'll make you stand out from the crowd, which is, ultimately, one of the major purposes of the kind of marketing we're trying to do.** The goal is to "uncommoditize" you, so you can compete on your wonderful value and your powerful relationships, not your price.

**Yours will be the only handwritten note your prospect or customer will receive that day, week, likely that month, and quite possibly that year.** They will remember you, and the memory will be warm and impressive. Nearly every person I send a note to brings it up to me some time later. It is a discussion point. They will think about you, and they will talk about you, and when the time comes, they will buy (more) from you.

**Handwrite notes because all people get anymore is email.** It's cold, high-tech, and highly interruptive. Your notes, on the other hand, are warm, impressive, and memorable. Let everyone else send email. You send your customers and prospects something they'll remember.

Send handwritten notes because they're incredibly thoughtful. They show your recipient that you took the time to sit down, write with pen and paper, and send your kind note to them. (These should only be kind, by the way. If you're mad, email!)

Whenever this topic comes up in my workshops, people start to nod their heads. They like the idea of working like this: slowly, and deliberately, and intelligently. Almost always, people say "I *used to* send handwritten notes." I tell them that today is the perfect day to start again.

When's the last time you got a handwritten note, on paper or stationery? Long time, right?

Same for your customers and prospects.

So, write them a note. You'll be the only one doing so.

### Some Quick Tips for Sending Effective Handwritten Notes

- Invest in a good pen. I like fountain pens, they're a hobby. (I have a lot of hobbies—including wine, pens, and travel—and nearly all of them are good for business!) But you can write with a ballpoint pen, or a rollerball, or a feather if you like. Get a pen you feel good using, something that's significant and makes you feel like a success. Something you want to reach for.

- A good pen demands proper paper. Don't get your name printed on the paper. But do get paper with a watermark on it. Write on the correct side of the paper, so that the watermark is readable by your recipient. Good paper is not inexpensive. Make this investment. It'll provide an exponential return, many times what you invest in the pen and paper.

- Get matching envelopes. Paper and envelopes should look the same.

- I send three to five notes every Friday. I like to close my week with this activity, the earlier the better. If I'm writing notes by 1 P.M., I know that my week will be over within an hour. I look back on the week, and consider who I've interacted with and who I'd like to reach again. Who do I want to know that I am thinking about them? Who would I like to tell that they have my support? Who do I want to do business with?

Who had a rough week and needs a pick-me-up? Who sent me an email and made me think that I'd like to build our relationship? Then I just pick a few of them and write.

- It doesn't matter what you write, as long as it's kind, positive, and thoughtful.
- If you send them at week's end, your recipients will get them toward the beginning of the following week, and you'll hear from them shortly thereafter. If you call them the following week, you'll have something wonderful to start the conversation with: "I sent you something in the mail . . ."

Why yes you did, you smart, thoughtful, wonderful person.

## Chapter Summary

Send handwritten notes. Stand out from the crowd. Be memorable. Grow revenue.

# 27 | Growth Technique #10: Communicate with Your High-Potential Small Customers (HPSCs)

Here is a powerful exercise I go through with my clients.

The purpose of this exercise is to take an honest look at your customer base and identify your customers with the highest growth potential. Once they are identified, you know exactly who to focus your communication on and who to really target with the techniques in this book.

Take a look at the diagram in Figure 27.1, which represents your entire customer base.

Let's work through this together now, from right to left.

Think about your biggest customers. These are the people who spend the most money with you. Write down how many of these customers you work with above the triangle and the combined revenue they account for below the triangle.

Moving to the center of your customer model: How many customers comprise your mid-size customers by volume? This is your next largest grouping of customers in terms of the amount of revenue they generate for you. Write down their quantity on top of the model and the total revenue they account for below.

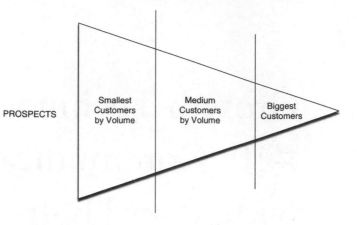

**Figure 27.1    The Customer Development Model**

Now for your smallest customers: How many little guys do you have? And what percentage of your revenue do they generate?

Finally, at the left of the model are your prospects. Approximately how many prospects do you have?

If you don't know the exact numbers, don't go off on a research expedition. Approximations are fine here.

Your customer development model should look something like that in Figure 27.2.

The company in Figure 27.2 is a $76 million business, with 24 customers that make up $25 million in revenues. This firm also has 125 mid-size

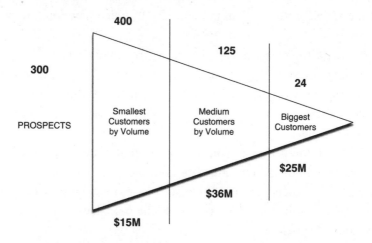

**Figure 27.2    Your Customer Development Model**

customers that account for $36 million in business. And, it has a whopping 400 customers that together represent just $15 million. This company also has 300 prospects.

Please fill in your own model before going further, because we're about to start the fun part!

Ask yourself: *Who can graduate to the right?*

Your business grows when you either add more customers into the model, or you grow business with existing customers (see Figure 27.3). So, let's think it through now: Which of your customers can move to the right?

How many of your medium-size customers can do enough additional business with you to graduate to become one of your biggest customers? Write the number of these customers by the arrow.

How many of your smallest customers can jump over the mid-size customers and go straight to being among your highest-revenue customers? Write down the number by that arrow.

How many of your smallest customers can become your mid-size customers, by volume?

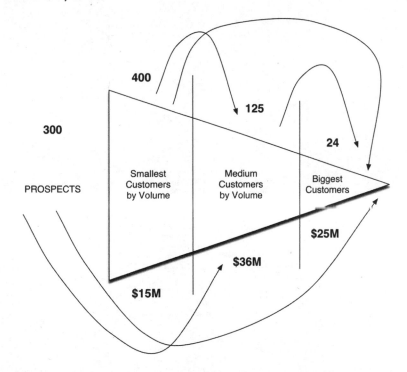

**Figure 27.3   Your Customer Development Model**

Now consider your prospects.

How many of your prospects have the ability to become your biggest customers? Write down the number by the arrow.

And how many prospects can become mid-size customers? Large customers?

How many small customers can graduate to the mid-size or large categories?

So, now, your model should look like the one in Figure 27.4.

The numbers in the circles are the customers you think can grow significantly to graduate into the groups of larger customers.

These are your high-growth-potential customers, or HGPCs.

The numbers I've used in the example are typical. Most firms can double the number of their largest customers! *This* is sexy.

They can also significantly grow their medium-size customers.

Now to the most important step.

Identify the people—*the humans*—that make up the customers in the circles. You may well have more than one contact per company. List them

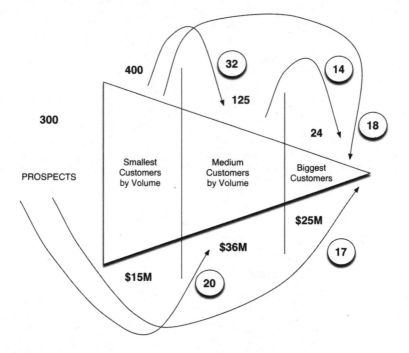

**Figure 27.4   Your Customer Development Model**

all. These customers are your lowest-hanging fruit in pursuit of revenue growth. This fruit hangs so low, in fact, that it's touching the blades of grass, and it can be knocked off—and deposited into your bank account—just by the breeze generated as you walk past it.

Once you have your list, simply focus your communications on those customers.

In particular, target testimonials from customers in a bigger spending group to your high-growth-potential customers.

In other words, communicate the testimonials from your largest customers to your high-growth-potential medium and small customers. Show them how good life is for your biggest customers. Show them how much your biggest customers benefit from your work, how much time they save, how you help to grow their business. Show them in your own big customers' words. *Make your smaller customers aspire to become your biggest customers.* The purpose of targeting testimonials this way is to create a desire from the smaller customers to become larger customers.

Also, use the "did you know" question liberally with these high-growth-potential customers. They can get much bigger; let's give them a map for doing so.

You've just identified your highest-potential customers.

Now it's time to help them spend more with you.

Communicate with them—especially them.

And watch your revenue grow.

## Chapter Summary

- Your high-growth-potential customers are the firms that can most easily spend more money with you.
- Identify them, and communicate with them.
- Don't forget about your prospects who can jump directly to being a mid-size customer or a large customer.
- Communicating testimonials from your largest, most successful customers is the most effective way to encourage smaller and mid-size customer to do more business with you. This kind of communication creates an *aspiration* to do more business with you.

# 28 | Growth Technique #11: Create Your Own Social Media—Relentlessly Grow Your Lists

A good list is one of the most powerful revenue growth tools a company has.

A list is valuable because it allows you to create your own social media.

If you're leading a small or mid-size company, and especially if you sell to other companies, your customers and prospects are not looking for you on social media. They are simply not deciding who to buy from based on anything anyone is going to write on Facebook or Twitter. Why focus on Facebook, where your customers and prospects are not looking for you, when you can be in their email inbox or on their desk, via a good list?

A list has many purposes, but its chief value to us within the scope of *The Revenue Growth Habit* is to allow you to communicate with many customers and/or prospects at once. It is the foundation on which your company-to-many communication is built. Without it, you really can't execute half of the effort that revenue growth requires.

## Where to Maintain Your List

Clients and audience members often ask me about the best place to maintain their list.

Short answer: It doesn't matter.

Slightly longer answer: Keep it where you like, but the simplest solution is almost always best. And the simplest solution for most people is the one you already have. In order of simplicity, the following are good places for your list:

- A spreadsheet. Why not? A spreadsheet gives you one field per column and a quick ability to sort and organize your data.
- An internal database you're already using. This can be whatever system you may have on your company server. It can be based on any of the platforms: Access, FileMaker Pro, or more sophisticated systems like Oracle or SQL.
- A cloud-based CRM like Salesforce.com if you'd like.
- My own list is in Infusionsoft, a cloud-based product designed for small companies with fewer than 10 employees.

I repeat: Start simply. A simple start that evolves is infinitely better than no start at all. Don't research these right now, either. Start your list. In today's era of instant information, too much action is put off in the name of research. It's not research, it's procrastination. (And I can define it so clearly because I'm well acquainted with it personally.)

If your list exists in one of the places just mentioned or somewhere else, just work on it where it is. No need to move it now. Build it first, move it (maybe) later.

## Components of a Good List

Your list should be made of human beings, not companies. We build relationships with people, not corporations, and most small and medium-size companies in the business-to-business space are in the relationship business. So focus your list on contacts, not companies. Here are the basic fields of a good list:

- Name
- Job title
- Company
- Physical address
- Phone
- Email

These are the most basic, most important items of information. You may want to add additional information like:

- Website
- LinkedIn profile
- Products purchased

Think of what's important to you, and add the fields to the list. If you don't use them, remove them. List building is not an exercise you finish. You will likely constantly be building, expanding, and adjusting your list.

In the next chapter we'll talk about powerfully categorizing and segmenting your list with a few extra fields.

## The Good List Core Four

A good list is made up of the following "core four" groups of people:

1. **Current customers:** Everyone your company is currently doing business with.
2. **Past customers:** These are people who used to buy from you but stopped.
3. **Current prospect:** Everyone who isn't a customer today but is thinking about becoming one. These are people you've had a buying conversation with. Perhaps they have a quote or a proposal from you. It's clear which product(s) or service(s) they are considering. They either know your prices, or soon will.
4. **Past prospects:** This is the hardest category to gather. These are people you discussed business with once, but they did not buy. You might find them in your old emails, call notes, or past quotes or proposals.

The first three types of people are relatively easy to start with. Gather them together, and start sending them value.

## Adding Others to Your List

A good list should be constantly growing. There are other ways to round out your list.

Consider the activities you can participate in where you come across people who can be added to your list:

- Trade shows
- Speeches
- Webinars
- Partnering with suppliers or customers

Further, you can acquire lists that are already assembled. Be cautious here; this is rarely a good investment.

Far more effective are resources I call "professional list builders" who can assemble lists of your prospects based on specific criteria like job title, industry, revenue size, and other attributes. Such companies employ researchers who manually assemble people and their contact information for your list. You'll be emailing these new prospects cold, however. They did not ask for your information, and spam laws are very strict.

## Assign a Keeper of the List

The list needs an owner, a maintainer, a keeper.

This is somebody who your staff can send the email signatures of customers and prospects to, who will input them into your list.

Make sure the identity of the list keeper is clear to everyone in your firm.

And give this person the authority to ask your customer-facing staff to regularly send contacts.

## Just . . . Start

So many people I've worked with hesitate to start sending value to their list because "it's not done yet."

It won't be.

Ever, hopefully.

It just needs to be started.

Even 100 people on a list are enough to start mailing to. Five hundred is better, and 1,000 is better still, but start with who you have—start with who there is.

They key is to get a starter group of people together and begin sending them your newsletters, testimonials, case studies, and so forth.

---

### Chapter Summary

- A good list is made of people, not companies, and is never finished and always expanding.
- Include personal information that will allow you to email, call, and send postal mail.
- A good list includes the following core of people: current customers, past customers, current prospects, and past prospects.
- Get a starter group together, and send them value.

---

# 29 | Growth Technique #12: Categorizing for Revenue Growth—How to Organize Your Lists

A list is the key to the second track of revenue growth. All of your one-to-many communications are only as effective as your list.

But a list's real power comes from the categories you include in it.

Data people call this segmentation, which I can accept. But sometimes this, is called slicing and dicing, as if we're making some kind of salsa. Just think of them as categories. If your list is in a spreadsheet, these are simply additional columns to allow you to quickly sort your list, select a group of email addresses, and send those people something valuable. If you're using a database or a CRM, there are probably several different places to utilize categories like this. Pick a field, or a group of fields, and stay consistent. The start is the key!

To determine your categories, think about the specific industries you work in and the kinds of people you sell to. Think about your geography. And also consider the size of the customers and prospects you sell to, as well as the amount they spend with you annually.

## Five Examples of List Categories

Here are five categories you might consider:

1. **Industry:** Because people in, say, the oil and gas industry care about different things than people in the airline industry. This way you can send value that people in each area care about. I would limit these to your top 5 or 10, with an "Other" listing to catch everyone who doesn't fit into your top ones. I would not make a list of 75 industries. Keep it simple, always.

2. **Job Title:** Again, list your top five, always including owners. Owners care about different things than everybody else. They care about total revenue, profits, and other big picture aspects of the company. Staff members care less about these things and more about their individual sales, for example, or their bonus amount. Technical people care about details and specifications. Purchasing professionals care about saving as much as possible. They care about these areas because they are evaluated on them. The beauty of the Revenue Growth Habit is that we send our customers and prospects help, information, and value based on what's important to them.

3. **Total Sales:** This is a range of revenue that each individual's company spends with you. So create four or five categories that are right for you. List a dollar range for your biggest customers, second biggest customers, and so on. We'll want to talk to our biggest customers in a different way and about different information than we would our smallest ones. The smaller customers aren't buying nearly as much as our bigger customers, for example, so we can likely teach them much more about what else they can buy from us.

4. **Annual Revenue:** You may want to address publicly traded customers or prospects differently than small mom-and-pop shops. So, add a category for revenue size, again using a few dollar ranges that make sense for your company.

5. **Geography:** If it matters to your work, use a category based on your customers' and prospects' locations.

If these work for you, terrific. If you have some other obvious categories of customers and prospects, put them to work.

## How to Use Categories

Here's the powerful part: With your list categories based on the categories we discussed here, you can:

- Send a quick tip or value item on profitable growth to all owners of companies valued at $10 million and up in the Northeast.
- Share a video on productivity with all of your purchasing managers in the building industry within companies larger than $100 million.
- Send a quick promotional offer to all engineers on your list from the auto industry.
- If you're in the consumer business and you've set appropriate categories, you can quickly select all moms who work who are also renting their homes.

Categories let you talk to subgroups on your list and share specific value that's interesting and compelling to them. You might think about multiple newsletters for multiple audiences, for example.

And one final reminder: On the company-to-many track, remember the general order of implementation: a core list first, which is then expanded as you have time. Then create a company newsletter for everyone. And only when you have a good handle on sending your newsletter our regularly and consistently, should you add additional actions to the company-to-many track.

---

### Chapter Summary

- List categories allow us to communicate with different people in different ways along our company to many track.
- Categorize your list based on your most important groupings of customers and prospects.
- With most of my clients, I like to use industry, job title, revenue size, and total sales.
- Sort your list by one or multiple categories to address specific value to specific groups of people.

# 30

# Growth Technique #13: Send a Wildly Valuable Newsletter to Your List

After you put together a starter list, which will be expanded and developed from now until the end of time, the first communication you should implement into your company-to-many track is a good newsletter for that list.

## Your Newsletter Should Be Brief

Keep your newsletter short; it should be readable in less than five minutes.

My weekly newsletter is called *The Evangelist Marketing Minute*. It comes out on Monday mornings and is always brief enough to read in less than 60 seconds. There are two reasons for this: First, I want readers to get value quickly, and I want them to know they will always find useful information in my newsletter that takes mere seconds to consume. Second, I don't like writing in long form, but I very much enjoy writing with brevity. And frankly, when I launched it a few years ago, I knew that if each edition took an hour, or hours, to write, I'd simply not do it every time. As it stands, I've never missed a Monday. Holidays, vacation days, and sick days, my readers have received value from me every Monday, for a couple hundred Mondays in a row now.

Go brief, and go on with your day.

And for goodness sake, don't make people click on a link in your newsletter to "continue reading" your story. Simplify their lives, improve their lives, don't complicate them.

## Your Newsletter Should Be Seen as Valuable

Your recipients should view your newsletter as being full of value.

Like all good marketing, it should help them, not sell to them.

It should improve their lives and work, as your products and services do.

If you approach your newsletter as a vehicle to convey value, the people on your list will look forward to it. They will read it, share it, and reference it. One of the best compliments I get is when readers tell me they collect my newsletters, print them, jot notes on them, and reference them frequently.

## Ideal Newsletter Frequency

A good starting point for your newsletter is every two weeks.

A lot of companies send monthly.

Monthly is enough for your readers to forget you, but not enough for them to remember you.

Twelve communications per year is not enough.

Weekly is an effective frequency, but a lot of people have a hard time generating good content that often.

Which brings us back to every two weeks. That's 24 newsletters per year. Send them on every other Monday, or Wednesday, or whatever day of the week suits you.

If you promise to publish at a consistent pace, you must deliver. It's better not to start a newsletter than to promise one every two weeks and not deliver it. That's letting your customers and prospects down. That's breaking your promise—not a good marketing technique.

Make a promise and keep it. I think you can keep the every-two-weeks promise.

## Newsletter Structure

After testing various formats and structures with clients, I've found that the most effective newsletter has three short sections.

### *First, Include an Article of Value*

This is a very brief written piece that helps your readers with something— anything, really—that's within your area of expertise. Think about common areas that your customers struggle with. What are they doing poorly, or incorrectly, or what can be improved? Now, write a paragraph or two on those items. Don't think too long, just write.

When I work with clients on this, we spend 30 minutes discussing these areas of improvement for their customers. We'll create a list of a dozen different topics, and two or three article titles for each. Then my clients have a laundry list of article topics to choose from when they sit down to write their newsletters. You can do the same thing right now, on your own.

Let's say, for example, your customers are retailers, and they don't demonstrate their equipment particularly well.

You might come up with several topics on how to demonstrate equipment well:

- Test-driving for sales.
- How demonstration location impacts equipment sales.
- Demonstrating to owners, demonstrating to engineers

That's three different newsletter articles, taking you through a full six weeks of articles if you're sending every two weeks.

Now think of another topic and two or three other article headlines.

Remember, each piece is brief and full of value. Think one or two paragraphs—that's it.

Use these articles to give people one tip, tool, technique, or takeaway. That's the goal: One helpful item, off the top of your head.

These articles should take you no more than 10 minutes to write.

You know your customers. You know where they can improve. Now, just write a few words about how. You can do this in your sleep.

### Next, Add a Testimonial

Go to your central collection of testimonials, and copy and paste one into your newsletter. Be sure to include the customer's name, job title, and company. This should take a few seconds.

### Finally, End with a Promotion

It can be a featured product, with a picture and link to your website. It can be a special discount. Perhaps it's an upcoming event you're promoting. Anything is fair game here. Ideally, this section includes a link to further information on whatever you're promoting. Give people a call to action, even if it's to reply to this email or to pick up the phone and call you. This might require five minutes.

That's three parts: a short article, a testimonial, and a featured product or promotion. That's it. That's the newsletter. Fast to write, quick to read, and extremely helpful to your readers.

## Total Time Investment

Once you get into a good rhythm with your newsletter—maybe by the third or fourth one—they should take you no more than 15 minutes to write. Every Monday I sit down at my computer first thing in morning, and I think about the things that happened last week. I think about my interactions with clients, audiences, and even the news. Did I read something interesting? Can I tie that information into helping my readers? Did somebody say something particularly interesting in one of my sessions that everyone should hear?

I pick something, and I write about it, and I send the newsletter.

As with all of this work, it doesn't matter what you write about, only that you write and send. *Most importantly, send.*

### Email or Snail Mail?

Sometimes I work with clients who have quite a number of customers and prospects who don't use email. In this case, print your newsletters, put them into an envelope, and mail them to those people. No downside to this, except the low cost of a stamp. Send it by email to everyone you can, and by snail mail to everyone you cannot email.

---

### Chapter Summary

- A good newsletter is the first tool to be added to your company-to-many track of communications.
- Every two weeks is an ideal frequency for your newsletter.
- The three parts of a good newsletter are: a short article or other valuable content, a testimonial, and a product or promotion.
- Write these in 15 minutes, not 90 minutes, and certainly not in three hours.
- The point is to help your customers and prospects. You help them everyday. Now, just write it down.

---

# 31 | Growth Technique #14: Growth by White Papers

A white paper is an educational document designed to help your customers and prospects.

In our case, a good white paper is nothing more than a collection of material you've already written.

If you're sending a newsletter every two weeks, as discussed in Chapter 30, then you'll have enough of those value articles—the first section of each of your newsletter—to collate into a white paper every quarter. Add some testimonials on facing pages so that they stand alone, and you'll have a nice 10-page white paper every three months.

There is no shame in repurposing content. In fact, there's only revenue, which is, for our purposes, the opposite of shame! Reuse everything you create as much as you can. People consume content in different ways, and we can't assume they've read every newsletter. And even if they have, research shows people need to see the same information at least seven times before they internalize it.

The last page of your white paper should contain your full contact details, and, if you wish, some promotional information about products you select or specials you're running. The material on this last page can change over time.

The key with white papers, as with all of your content, is to get them in front of customers.

Make sure customers and prospects see them.

The best way to communicate your white papers is one-on-one by email. It's just another reason to contact people who can buy from you. "We just put together this white paper on effective product demonstrations on the show floor, and I thought of you. Please accept this white paper with my compliments. By the way, how's your business going? Please let me know if you need any more X or Y or Z."

Another terrific way to send white papers to customers and prospects is along the company-to-many track. Select a number of people from your list—or just select everybody—and send them your white paper as a special mailing.

As with most of what's in this book, there's no wrong way to do this.

The key, as always, is simply to *do this*.

---

### Chapter Summary

- A white paper is simply another tool to add value for your customers and prospects.
- Feel free to repurpose material from your newsletters. Just collate the content, package it in a white paper, and add testimonials and a promotional page at the end.
- Then, as with all of the high-value content you create, make sure that customers and prospects see it.
- White papers are equally effective on the one-on-one and the company-to-many tracks of communications.

# 32 | Growth Technique #15: Turning Trade Shows into Revenue

Here's my simple advice to my closely held clients about succeeding at trade shows.

Let everybody else focus on their products and services.

*You* focus on your happy customers, who are the peers of the people wandering through the trade show.

Instead of handing attendees your product catalog, hand them a catalog of happy customers.

Hand them case studies.

Hand them books of testimonials.

It's very difficult to defend against happy, successful peers. And the attendees will want that too, for themselves.

Have things printed and prepared, and say to attendees you meet, "You know, I work with somebody who's similar to you. Similar business, similar size. He has told me recently that working with us saves him from having to run an entire second shift. That's about a million dollars in annual savings, and he has been with us for 25 years. Here's the case study about this customer. How about we talk about providing you with the same kind of value?"

Practice this language. Get comfortable with it.

Ask about the attendee's company. Then say, "That's really interesting, I have several customers just like you. One of them tells us that 23% of his annual revenue growth is a direct result of our work together. Now I think we should talk about doing the same thing for you."

Be bold. These stories are the truth. These are your stories. This is your work. Be bold, you deserve to be. In fact, you owe it to these trade show attendees, who are here to learn and improve, to tell them clearly how you can help them. (Which is very different, by the way, than telling them about your products.)

You will be the only one at the trade show doing this. You will stand out like a blossoming cherry tree in a forest full of oaks.

Let your competitors commoditize themselves and talk about their specifications and technologies.

You stand out. You stand apart.

Really, this is the mindset shift discussed in Chapter 4, implemented in the trade show environment.

In your booth, don't use large photos of your products.

Instead, use pictures of your customers. The happy people. Their company logos. Their buildings. Their products!

You will probably have multiple people working your booth. Make sure they carefully review your case studies well in advance. Practice these conversations with each other. Role play them.

Talk about your customers, not your products and services.

That's how to turn trade shows into revenue growth shows!

---

### Chapter Summary

- At trade shows, talk about your happy, successful customers, not your products and services.
- Have testimonials and case studies to hand out to attendees.
- Ask attendees about their business or work, and tell the story of a successful customer of yours in a similar business.
- A focus on products at trade shows commoditizes you. A focus on happy customers makes you stand out.

# 33

## Growth Technique #16: Host an Unforgettable Event for Customers and Prospects

Recently I worked with the owner of a print label manufacturer and I was interviewing his customers, predominantly print distributors. One of them had a terrific story to tell.

This woman, a highly successful business owner who sold mostly locally, gathered her best customers and hired a private jet. She loaded her customers on board the plane, and flew them down to my client, who was expecting them. He showed them around the facility, took them to dinner, and then everyone got back on the plane and went home.

I asked her how much she spent on this event.

She said about $20,000 for the jet.

I asked how much revenue it generated.

She answered that over the next years; her total business with these customers added up to well in excess of 100 times that amount.

*That* is an excellent investment.

That evening is easily one of the most memorable moments her customers have ever had in business. They most likely still remember it clearly. After all, how many times do small business owners get to travel on a private jet?

Here's another story, this one is my own.

At least once a year, I like to have private events for my clients, who are owners of private companies between $5 million and $2 billion. I like to gather a group of a couple dozen of them, about half of whom are customers, and half of whom are prospects to me. I do this because I want the happy clients talking to people who are not yet working with me. The day that people arrive, I host a cocktail reception, or I take them out to a nice dinner. The next day, we have a working session, where I teach my latest intellectual property on revenue growth. We spend a day working together at a first-class facility like the Four Seasons or the Ritz, and they get meet and mingle with highly successful peers.

There's no cost to attend, but the price of admission is that everyone must be an owner or the spouse of the owner. This is my market, and as much as I'd like to entertain the colleagues of my target clients, there's a time and a place for that, and this isn't it.

We stop the workday at about 2 P.M., and then I hire transportation to take everyone to a singular experience.

For the most recent event I hosted, we were driven to the top auto dealership of exotic sports cars in Chicago. There were drinks and food, and my clients and prospects not only had their pictures taken next to some of the most expensive cars on the planet but sitting behind the wheel of them! Many of my people got to test drive these amazing vehicles as well. Think they'll remember that?

Of course, I spoke very briefly, thanking everyone for attending. More important, I arranged for two very happy clients to say a few words to those in attendance. Talk about evangelist marketing!

I don't know what this event will return in terms of the growth of my business, but I know two things: It will be healthy, but even if it isn't, I had a blast and so did my guests.

Here are some rules-of-thumb for your private events:

**Make them memorable.** The more interesting and exciting they are, the better. And you don't have to spend a lot of money to create an interesting event. Be creative. Use your imagination. Can you arrange for a behind-the-scenes tour of a sporting facility, for example? Depending upon your customer demographic, many places are happy to partner with you to host your event in exchange for the exposure to your group.

**Mix customers and prospects.** The goal is to orchestrate the former to sing your praises to the latter. Instead of *us* communicating customer testimonials, these kinds of events allow the happy customers to do it themselves.

**Consider adding on to an existing, much larger event.** These kinds of things work great at industry conventions, if you specialize in one vertical or another. Everyone is already there, nobody needs to travel, and, even better, a buzz builds around your invitation-only event. People start asking each other throughout the days leading up to it if they will also be attending your event. People will *aspire* to be at your event. It will be dripping with value and exclusivity.

When I worked exclusively with consumer electronics companies, I held these kinds of private events at the Consumer Electronics Show in Las Vegas every year. They got so popular that people asked me to organize small-group meetings of peers throughout the year. Twist my arm! My customers and prospects voluntarily gathering with me quarterly to discuss my work and value? That wasn't terrible.

---

## Chapter Summary

- Private events are a terrific and fun way to grow your business.
- Make them memorable, creative, and exclusive.
- Invite a mix of customers and prospects so as to allow happy customers to sing your praises to prospects.
- If you specialize in working with certain categories of businesses, consider adding on your invitation-only event. This eliminates the need for your customers and prospects to take a special trip.
- Let the competition host dinners. You host singular events that your market will remember attending forever and talk about for years to come.

# 34 | Growth Technique #17: Speak(er) the Truth—You're the Expert

When you exhibit at a trade show, you are one of many with a booth or table, just like everybody else.

When you speak at a trade show, you're the expert, and everybody is (literally) looking to you for guidance, leadership, and experience.

You're teaching people.

You're helping people.

You're demonstrating your value.

People sit in the audience, imagining what it's like to buy from you.

People think with you. They learn from you. Hopefully, they take your advice and recommendations back to their business and think about you for days or maybe weeks after your presentation.

Think that happens when you are one of the exhibitors on the trade show floor?

## Speeches to Business

Of all of the techniques in this book, this is the one I use personally to grow my business the most.

There is nothing that grows my company more, or faster, than speeches.

But I run a consulting company, so I get to talk about my areas of expertise. I can speak anywhere where my customers and prospects gather. I work predominantly with owners and presidents of closely held businesses between $23 million and $250 million in revenue, with some exceptions that are significantly larger firms. But my concepts apply across industries, so the organization doesn't really matter to me. I can help any owner in any industry, so long as he or she has a customer-facing staff to do the simple communications work laid out in these pages.

If your business sells products or services, the key is for you to speak where you customers gather.

Which means: If you're an attorney, or accountant, or real estate agent, consider local organizations like chambers of commerce, Kiwanis, and Rotary and Lions clubs. Local companies gather here, and these rooms are probably at least partially filled with people who can buy from you.

If you are in a specific niche industry, like construction, or oil equipment, or print manufacturing, you need to be in rooms where your prospects and customers go. This probably limits you to various industry associations. But there are likely several of them, and you probably know what they are right now.

Make a quick list, and start contacting the people who run these associations, offering yourself as an expert who would be happy to help their members and audiences.

## How to Write Speeches

If you've been exhibiting at a particular trade show for some time, simply contact the organizers or the association executive director, and offer your expertise as a speaker. You'll need a topic and a brief description before you reach out to them. Creating your speech topic is the same process as coming up with topics for your newsletter:

- What do your customers struggle with that you can help them with?
- Where do they waste valuable time?
- Where in their sales process do they lose customers? (Where is the leak in their revenue hose?)

- What internal efficiencies are they lacking?
- How's the record keeping?
- Is their accounting lagging?
- What about their internal communication?

Come up with a list of issues that your customers are dealing with. *Each one of these can be a speech.* Or, you can simply combine them all into one all-encompassing session.

Now, under each, write down three to five solutions to the problem. These become your main points.

Write a few sentences under each solution or main point.

Now add a decent introduction and closing, and you're done. There's your speech. Total time investment: 60 to 90 minutes.

---

## Chapter Summary

- Consider speeches as a way to rise above the competition, and stand out at crowded trade shows.
- List organizations and associations where your customers and prospects gather, and contact their executive leadership offering your value as a presenter.
- Create your speech topics by listing issues your customers are struggling with and your proposed solutions. These are your speeches.
- Don't perfect, don't dwell, just go help people and book new business!

# 35

## Growth Technique #18: Conduct Webinars That Bring New Business

Webinars are speeches you give at your computer.

And your audience gets to enjoy your expertise at their computers.

Webinars feature your voice over your presentation slides. They are effective for demonstrating your value to customers and prospects with very little financial or time investment. A good webinar runs 30 to 60 minutes. You can use your topic list from the last chapter for your webinars.

See how things get repurposed?

The topics you write about in your newsletter get turned into a white paper.

The same topics can be combined to create your speech.

And the material in your speech is exactly the same material in your webinar.

### How to Put on a Good Webinar

Since the webinar content is the same as what you'll create for your speech with the guidelines from the last chapter, let's look at the logistics of doing webinars:

- This is a company-to-many activity, because you will invite all of the people on your list. With speeches, the organization or association is responsible for getting the audience into seats. With webinars, it is your responsibility.

- Send multiple emails inviting people to your webinar. Five invitations over the two weeks leading up to the webinar is not too many.

- Use a service like GoToWebinar to run your session. This is the one I use. It allows you to create an invitation page with a sign-up form, and then it does all the work for you. You get a link to place in your email invitations, which your customers and prospects click on to register.

- There is a specific date and time that your webinar occurs (you choose), it's appointment viewing, and only those who register can participate.

- You should also record your webinar—which is a matter of pushing a button on the GoToWebinar interface. This creates a video file, which you can repurpose on your website and as a high-value item to email to customers and prospects later.

- Once the webinar ends, you can use a feedback form to solicit information from your audience. Ask them about anything you'd like, including their thoughts on your webinar. *Be sure to ask about their business, their work, or their needs for your products and services.*

- Following your webinar, send a follow-up email to everyone and include the slides you used.

## Chapter Summary

- Webinars are speeches done at your computer.
- Use an established, well-known service, and send invitations to your list aggressively.
- Since you're helping people and not selling on your webinar, do not hesitate to promote it vigorously.
- Record your session for later distribution.
- Don't forget to have fun!

# 36

# Growth Technique #19: How to Grow Your Business with Videos

Videos may be used along either communication track—one-on-one or company-to-many. They add a third dimension to the value you provide—people can see you instead of just read you. Videos allow people to visualize you, your customers, and products. Videos differentiate you from the competition and help you stand out from the crowd, which is the point of all the marketing work in this book.

## Rules for Effective Revenue Growth Videos

**The best videos are short.** Think two minutes or less. Any longer, and you're going to lose the viewer.

**Informal beats formal.** A relaxed setting beats a studio setting. A real-world background beats an all-white or all-black background.

**Help your audience; demonstrate your value.** Just like every other communication technique in this part of the book, we want videos to demonstrate your great value to your customers and prospects. You're not pitching or selling in your videos. You're simply helping people.

185

**Upload your videos to YouTube.** That's where videos live. There are other video hosting sites, but YouTube is obviously the biggest and best known. From there, you can share them, place them on your website, and get them to customers and prospects.

## What to Create Videos On

You can create videos on a wide range of topics. Let's talk about some.

### *Customer Case Studies*

There are three ways to do case studies on video:

1. **You can tell the customer's story on camera.** Just go through a case study while looking at the camera. Tell your viewers about the problem this customer was having when she came to you, what she bought from you to resolve the problem, the great value she received, and share a testimonial at the end. "This customer tells me that. . . . "
2. **The customer can tell his own story on camera.** Think of this as a mini testimonial video. Just ask your customer some questions about what he liked best about working with you and how it helps him.
3. **You and your customer can explain the case study together.** You'd both be on camera, and you would discuss how you work together. You can talk about what the customer buys; he can talk about how working with you has helped him and what's improved since he has come to you. Frankly, you can discuss whatever is on your mind.

The value of all of these customer stories on video is that they allow prospects to imagine themselves working with you. Moreover and even better: These videos will create an *aspiration* to work with you.

### *Teaching Moments*

Go back to your topics list for your newsletter value articles that we discussed in Chapter 30.

Every article you've ever written—or plan to write—can also be a video.

Talk about the issues your customer base struggles with, and help them with one issue at a time.

Pick a problem that many customers deal with. For example, many customers are so busy they do not respond to *their* customers in a timely manner. You might create a 90-second video that starts by describing the problem, then suggest three quick, simple solutions to this issue. You may tell people to allow for 30 minutes at the end of their day to return all outstanding phone calls. Or perhaps send a quick email immediately to everyone you cannot call back right away, telling them when you'll call. Things like this.

If you give it 10 minutes right now, you can come up with a dozen common issues your customers are struggling with, and solutions to suggest to them on video.

### Telling Your Story

Videos are a terrific platform to tell your fascinating story: the story of your company, the story of your family, or the story of your life. What brought you to this work? What's special about the history of your firm? Why do you do this work? What's important to you about your customers' experience? What do you teach your people, your colleagues, to focus on? Use video to help you connect with your market and to tell them exactly what is special about your journey up to this moment.

### Product Demonstrations and Tips

As much as I hesitate to tell you to create videos focused on your products, it's a useful technique *if you focus on the product's value to customers*. Go through the top three features of a product, detailing how they help your customers. Don't focus on the technology but on its value to the people who buy it from you. "Customers tell us this feature allows them to install our products a lot faster than the competition's stuff."

## How to Create Good Videos

To create videos, you can use a good high-definition camcorder or your smartphone. If you have a smartphone that was released in the last two years, the high-definition video cameras that are built in are quite good. And the advantage of capturing video on your phone is easy uploading to the Internet for sharing.

The key to a good video is, frankly, the audio. It must be crisp, clear, and not drowned out by background noise.

If you're in a quiet room, the built-in microphone is fine.

But if there's noise, get yourself a lavalier microphone that clips onto your shirt, blouse or lapel. There are even lavaliere mics for your smartphone now!

If you're so inclined, hire a camera operator, or enlist your spouse or child to help you.

But a tripod will do the job also.

Remember, we want effective, not polished and highly professional.

## How to Share Your Videos with Customers and Prospects

You can get your high-value, highly effective videos to customers in the following ways:

- **One-on-one, by email.** Make sure your sales and customer service people have the links to your videos, so they can use them as a highly effective tool for making contact with people who can buy from you. "Rita, a number of my customers have been asking about product demonstration at retail recently, I put together this 90-second video to help them. I thought you might find it of value."
- **Company-to-many mailing, specifically to distribute your videos.** "Here's a video we recently put together about our favorite time management technique for sales rep agencies. Please enjoy it with our compliments."
- **Company-to-many, via your newsletter.** Make your video the featured value item, replacing the article at the beginning.

## Chapter Summary

- Helpful, highly valuable videos help you to rise above the noise and stand out from the competition.
- Create videos featuring customer case studies, product demonstrations, or the presentation of your story.
- Good videos are brief, casual (not formal), and full of value for people who watch them.
- Share your videos one-on-one or company-to-many, via special video mailings, or simply embed them into your newsletter.

# 37 | Growth Technique #20: Public Relationships— How to Leverage the Media for Revenue Growth

Years ago, in the mid-2000s, at the height of the consumer electronics boom, I was a syndicated technology columnist for the *Chicago Tribune*. My column ran in more than 300 publications around the world.

Because of this, I received "pitches," or marketing, from thousands of public relations people.

They wanted me to cover their products, so they sent me a never-ending stream of press releases, review requests, and product details. In general, there was a lot of "please, please, please!"

Here was the problem: The products—smartphones, shrinking laptops, tablets, flat-panel TVs—were wonderful. The marketing, however, was atrocious.

It became obvious to me that some of the biggest and best-known companies on the planet succeeded in spite of their marketing, not because of it. World-class products, often with tens of millions of dollars in research behind them, were being marketed impersonally by 23-year-old PR people who didn't know, didn't care, and didn't follow up.

The vast majority of these PR people pitched journalists en masse, by the thousands. They sent us terrible press releases, which compelled or interested nobody, not even them. Their marketing focused on technical specifications, statistics, speeds, and sizes, but never benefits to the customer. Nobody ever talked about how their products improved people's lives, which, of course, these products did in spades.

Among this massive group of PR people who communicated with me daily, but who I mostly didn't know and never met, there were a handful of people who did something different.

They took the time to build a relationship with me.

They got to know me, what I covered, and what I was interested in.

They talked to me. Sometimes, we met for lunch or coffee.

These people tried harder than the others, and they worked smarter.

For these people who built a relationship with me, I bent over backwards to get their pitches into the newspaper.

Sometimes I would help them reshape their pitch so that my editor, the gatekeeper to coverage for these PR folks, would be more inclined to run their news.

On rare occasions, and only with these people, I would help them rewrite their releases so that they would be accepted.

They built a relationship; they got in the paper.

It's the same for you.

Today, I help my clients get coverage in their local and industry media.

The catalyst for such coverage is a relationship.

Help them before you need their help.

Read their work, and offer an opinion of value *to them, the members of the media*. Make suggestions and recommendations that are in their best interests, not necessarily yours.

Let them know they are free to contact you if they ever need anything in your areas of expertise (which is your company's products, or your educational training, or your specific work within your company).

Build a relationship.

Then, when your relationship is strong, make your pitch.

Let them know you're coming to them first.

Tell them about your family business, the generations that have come before you. Tell them your story.

More than likely, they'll cover it.

This cannot be rushed.

Take your time.

Help the media.

And the media will help you.

## Your Media Plan

1. **Identify five local mainstream journalists—newspaper writers, radio hosts, TV news reporters or anchors.** We're looking for five media members who would be interested in covering your company, or your story.
2. **Next, identify five different media members who write in industry publications.** These are frequently association magazines or newsletters. We want outlets that your customers and prospects read. It's one thing to advertise, but a reporter telling your story is far more effective. It's a third-party endorsement. They could be writing about anyone, and they're choosing to write about you.
3. **Start developing relationships with these 10 people.** Help them. Send your opinion on pieces they've written. Compliment their writing. Be nice. You know, be friendly.
4. **When you feel your relationship is strong enough, suggest that perhaps they may be interested in covering your firm and your story.**
5. **The key to media coverage is not that you get it, but what you do with it once you get it.** Articles and TV and radio pieces are fleeting. They're gone far faster than an Internet-based article. You must capture your press coverage, and communicate it. Create a PDF, or a recording, and send it to customers and prospects as a special mailing. Use it one-on-one and also in company-to-many communications like your newsletter, or simply a special one-off mailing emphasizing your recent coverage.

So, the success of your media campaign comes down to two words: Relationships. And communication.

The behaviors required to succeed with the media are pretty much identical to those required to succeed in business.

## Chapter Summary

- Local media and industry media are communications platforms underutilized by small and mid-size businesses.
- Just as with your customers, success with the media requires the careful development of relationships.
- The key to turning media coverage into business is to communicate that coverage to your list of customers and prospects.

# 38 | Growth Technique #21: Price Increases Are a Growth Technique!

Small and mid-size companies are often uncomfortable raising their prices. As a result, they don't change their prices for years. Sometimes, when a vendor increases prices of raw materials, small and mid-size companies will begrudgingly and uncomfortably raise their prices by exactly that amount, passing the increase on to the customer. But no additional net profit is gained, because so many small and mid-size companies are reluctant to ask.

"Our customers will leave us," they predict.

This is actually not true.

I often ask my clients' customers what they'd do if my clients' prices went up a point or two?

The answer: nothing.

They've been with you for years, or decades, for a reason.

They trust you. They value you. They depend on you. You make them money. You help them retain their customers. You help them look good. You're friends. Some of them think of you as family.

You don't leave relationships like that over 1 or 2%.

In 2014, the inflation rate in the United States was 1.58%, according to the U.S. Bureau of Labor Statistics.

In 2013, it was 1.59%.

In 2012, it was 2.93%.

In 2011, it was 1.63%.

In 2010, it was 2.63%.

In 2009, it was nearly 0.

But in 2008, it was 4.28%.

And in 2007, it was 2.08%.

We could keep going, and going, and going.

My point is, your customers won't leave you over gradual, small, but consistent price increases.

The trouble occurs when you don't increase prices at all for 10 years, and then you can't go on like this any longer, and you jack them up significantly all at once. That's when people notice.

If, conversely, you increase your prices by 0.5% or 1% on a regular basis, say every year or two, chances are people won't even notice. In fact, they *expect* for this happen. It's the way of the world. Everybody's prices increase regularly. McDonald's, Starbucks, and admission to the Disney Parks goes up in price consistently. The cost of automobiles, airline tickets, and food regularly increases also. We're used to this. We live in this environment. But small and mid-size companies, for some reason, fear price increases.

To be clear: I'm not talking about raising your prices by 5% or 10% in one dramatic swoop. No, this would cost you business. I'm talking about gradually getting to those percentages, over years of much smaller increases. Slow, small, but steady.

Often, my clients have been agonizing about a price increase before they meet me.

We talk it through.

Then I ask their customers what they'd do if my client's prices were to go up.

Then my clients listen to the audio recordings and absorb more encouragement and motivation from me.

Then, carefully, cautiously, wincing and cringing, they raise their prices by 0.5% to 1%.

And you know what happens? (Every time so far . . .)

Nothing.

Customers don't even notice.

Ninety-nine percent of their customers say nothing, and 1% complain. That 1% would have complained anyway, about something else, even if there weren't a price increase. Do you think the complainers leave? Almost never. They complain a bit, then they go on with their lives.

And clients go on to pocket the new profits.

Price increases are glorious because they are pure profit.

There are no additional costs to incur in a price increase.

Why do you deprive yourself of what everyone expects you to do already?

Raise your prices.

Enjoy the profits.

You deserve them.

---

## Chapter Summary

- You are much more uncomfortable with small, steady price increases than your customers are.
- Raise prices by 0.5% to 1% repeatedly, over the years.
- Most customers don't even notice. A tiny minority will complain, but the vast majority of them will stay with you, anyway.
- Price increases go straight to the bottom line.

# 39 | Growth Technique #22: The Single, Most Important Website Edit for Revenue Growth

Take a look at your website.

Who does it talk about? You? Or your customers?

Almost always, the websites of small and medium-size privately held companies are completely about the companies themselves, with almost no information about their customers.

Here's the same question, asked a different way:

Does your website focus on your products and services or the value you bring to your customers?

Does it profile you and your products, or does it profile happy, successful customers?

Here is the single, most important website change you can make to grow your business:

Shift its focus to your customers.
Start telling customer stories instead of product and service stories.

In Chapter 4 we talked about the most critical mindset shift you need to grow your business quickly: Instead of focusing your mind and your conversation on the products and services you sell, focus on the tremendous ways you help your customers.

This is also the most important website edit you can make: Focus less on your capabilities and your products and services, and talk about your customers.

Here are three concrete steps to take:

1. **Add a testimonial to every page, over time.** Since you will get multiple testimonials every time you ask your customers for feedback about why they're with you—following my model in Chapter 17 you will now have many testimonials to place on your website. It's okay if you use them multiple times. Obviously, don't worry about getting a testimonial onto every page immediately. Just copy and paste a few at time, one per page. Spend five minutes or less a day, and move on. In parallel, create a testimonials page where you have a running list of endorsements.

2. **Add your case studies to your website.** You know how to write them now (see Chapter 20). They're never longer than one page. Add them as web pages or PDF files, to various pages on your site. Create a case studies page that has a running collection of your customer profiles.

3. **This is key: Reorient your home page around your customer success stories.** Many websites feature sliders on the home page, which rotate through facts about the company or facts about its products. I don't mind sliders. But focus them on your customers. One customer per slide, with a photo of the person, a testimonial, and a link to what the customer bought from you. That's right, each slider should focus on one item or service each customer purchased, with a link to that item. This way, it's not you talking about you products and services, it's your customers.

Do not wait until you have two weeks to do this perfectly. Do not hire a web design firm to do this for you from start to finish. I want *you* to make these updates, one at a time. If you can't update your site, email one testimonial to your IT person or your web designer with instructions to place it on a particular web page. Tomorrow, or next week, send another. Then another. Like this. Take the pressure off your shoulders; you have enough problems. This is not one of them. This is a good thing. Small improvements lead to big revenue growth.

## Chapter Summary

- The most impactful improvement you can make to your website is to reorient it around your happy customers.
- Focus on their endorsements and successes with you by populating your website with testimonials and case studies.
- Aim to have a different testimonial on every page of your site, but place them one at a time, over extended periods of time.
- Organize your home page around rotating happy customers. Include links to the specific products or services your specific customers have purchased. Of course, include their testimonials.

# 40

## Growth Techniques by Job Title

Now that we've reviewed all 22 revenue growth techniques, let's break down the ideal actions by job title. These are the best actions for the most common customer facing professionals in your firm.

Basically, sales and customer service people should engage in the one-on-one activities, and the marketing manager, or whoever is playing quarterback on the company-to-many track of your communications, should orchestrate those communications that are sent to your list.

Managers and executives should spend their few minutes of daily action helping their people execute their actions.

### Owners and Upper Management
- The best thing you can do is to spend your 15 minutes a day helping your team execute their 15 minutes a day.
- The second most effective use of your time is to make phone calls, as discussed in Chapter 24.
- Finally, feel free to pick and choose any of the one-on-one techniques detailed in this section of the book. An owner or executive calling a customer for a testimonial is extremely impressive and flattering, for example.

*Sales and Customer Service Managers*
- Help your team execute.
- Hold your people accountable, which we will discuss in greater detail in the next part of the book.
- Share your people's successes with everyone to create a powerful flow of positive energy.
- Engage in any one-on-one activities that strike you as interesting.

*Outside Salespeople*
- Collect testimonials.
- Communicate testimonials.
- Communicate case studies.
- Ask the "did you know" question.
- Ask for referrals.
- Communicate with your high-growth-potential customers.
- Send handwritten notes.
- Follow up on quotes or proposals.
- Send your contacts to your marketing manager or whoever is maintaining your list within your firm.

*Inside Salespeople and/or Customer Service People*
- Ask the "did you know" question.
- Follow up on quotes.
- Collect testimonials.
- Communicate case studies.
- Ask for referrals.
- Send handwritten notes.
- Follow up on quotes or proposals.
- Send your contacts to your company's list keeper.

*Marketing Manager or Company-to-Many Track Quarterback*
- Maintain and grow the company's list.
- Send a newsletter every two weeks (start with these first two items first, and add on only when you get comfortable with the newsletter).
- Categorize your list.
- Create a white paper and distribute it.
- Incorporate your testimonials and case studies into your trade shows.
- Work on hosting a fabulous event for customers.
- Help an executive at your firm speak in front of audiences of customers and prospects.

- Organize and conduct webinars for customers or prospects.
- Create powerful revenue growth videos.
- Develop relationships with the media for coverage.
- Edit your website so that it focuses more on customers and less on your product and service details.

# PART

FOUR

# Executing the Plan

# 41

## Action Is Everything

You now have 22 specific communication techniques that will grow your revenue.

Which one will you do today?

Which one tomorrow?

Nothing happens without action.

Without action there are only unfulfilled plans and dreams.

There is logic and information but no results.

There is fear, procrastination, perfection, but there is no peace of mind, accomplishment, or resulting joy.

Frankly, without action, there is only wasted time.

The goal of this entire book is revenue growth so that you can improve your life, and the lives of your family, your customers, and your prospects. Remember all those people we discussed in Part Two of this book who deserve to get additional value from you? And all those people—yourself, first and foremost—who deserve to have your business grow? That's what this is about. This work will improve your life because it will grow your business. And in doing so, you'll improve the lives and companies of your customers and prospects. Isn't that worthy of a few minutes of action daily?

The work is easy, fast, and incredibly valuable to everyone involved. The work is righteous.

But the work must be done.

We must take action.

This final, shortest part of the book is about the action.

---

**Chapter Summary**

Select one of the 22 techniques just detailed and try it. If you like it, and it works, do it again. If not, try something else.

---

# 42 | How Perfection and Procrastination Kill Revenue

Too much revenue is lost to perfection and procrastination, which are nearly inextricable from one another.

Your products need to be perfect.

But your communications do not.

Your revenue growth communication—the techniques you will be implementing from this book—depend far more on quantity than quality.

*The more that people hear from you, the more they will buy from you.* It's a direct, positive correlation. It's impossible to make the opposite argument: That people buy more when they don't hear from you. If you're not communicating with your customers and prospects, you're out of sight, which also means you're out of mind, which means the business you deserve is going to your competition.

So, we must communicate. We must take action. And as we discussed in Part Two, this kind of direct-to-customer-and-prospect communication is often perceived as high risk. The risk of failure is perceived to be high. What if they reject me? What if they turn me down? Also, I'm so busy with customer requests. I have to fix their problems. I don't have time for this.

We procrastinate.

And thanks to the high perceived risk of rejection, we delay communication in an effort to perfect it.

*We only get one chance with this customer.* That's not true, there's a reason they've been with you for years, or decades.

*We better get it exactly right, or else they'll leave us.* The competition calls on them regularly, and every time, they make a decision to stay with you. You think they're going to leave if your high-value communication is only 85% ready instead of 100%? (Only you will know that 15% is missing, by the way. The customer or prospect will never know. Which means that last bit of perfecting we delay so much action for is completely dysfunctional. Nobody will know it's not perfect except for you.)

It is safer to not take action. So we put it off, we come up with reasons to wait. We can't be rejected or refused if we don't execute, so we procrastinate.

Listen to me carefully: Every one of the 22 communication techniques detailed in this book is designed to help your customers and prospects while generating additional revenue for you. These approaches are not about selling harder or more. They're about helping your customers and prospects more, which means there is rarely, if ever, any rejection or failure.

The worst of it, really, are customers unsubscribing from your newsletter.

There is nothing to be uncomfortable with here, because you are helping people.

The only failure is not doing this work.

The only failure is not communicating your value to these good people who wish to pay you for it.

In not communicating, in delaying communication, you are letting down your family, your colleagues, your customers, your prospects, and worst of all, yourself. *That's* failure.

Don't procrastinate on this work, there are too many people to help.

Don't have meetings to plan your action. Just take your action.

Don't agonize over this effort. Agony doesn't grow business.

Don't try to make it perfect, it doesn't need to be. *It won't ever be.*

Just move. Just communicate your value to people who can buy it.

Choose a technique described here, and try it.

That's the start.

Tomorrow, try another.

That's the repeating.

Now you're applying discipline, intentionality, to grow your revenue.

You are starting to create your revenue growth habit.

The start is the thing.

It's time to start.

---

### Chapter Summary

- Too much revenue is lost to perfection and procrastination.
- In revenue growth, quantity trumps quality; the more that people hear from you, the more they will buy.
- There is no wrong way of doing this. There is no failure. The only failure is to not do the work.
- Starting and repeating make up the simple discipline required to grow your business.

# 43 | Why 15 Minutes? Because It's Enough to Grow Your Business Dramatically

Each of the 22 revenue growth techniques listed in this book can be executed in a few minutes a day. Some of the techniques require a single email, much of which consists of copied-and-pasted text. That's seconds a day, and you're growing your revenue.

So, why 15 minutes?

Because it is easy. Fifteen minutes starts and ends quickly. It's relatively painless.

Fifteen minutes is difficult to overthink. You can't, really, because if you do, you'll be preparing for action longer than actually taking it.

It's also really fast. Even *you* have 15 minutes a day.

As such, 15 minutes is difficult to avoid. In fact, it's pretty much embarrassing to avoid.

Basically, I decided on 15 minutes because I needed an easily acceptable time frame for my clients' incredibly busy salespeople and customer service people. If I created a system that required an hour a day, I knew it wouldn't get done. I needed something that was impossible to argue with or resist.

Here's the biggest reason I went with 15 minutes a day: It's enough to create a new habit, which is what we're doing here.

The habit is the key.

It's the point where you stop thinking about it, and do it automatically.

One action a day, one communication a day, executed boldly, as a matter of course.

Just as you drink your coffee in the morning, or eat your lunch midday, you will take one of the proactive communication actions each day.

It will become a habit. For you, your colleagues, and your management.

Snowflakes to a blizzard.

Raindrops to a tsunami.

Communications to revenue.

A habit for revenue growth!

---

### Chapter Summary

Fifteen minutes a day is fast, easy, difficult to avoid, and enough time to establish a new revenue growth habit. It also happens to grow your sales dramatically.

# 44

## Introducing the 15-Minute Marketing® Planner

Here is the simple tool you'll use to plan and execute your marketing. See Figure 44.1.

### The 15-Minute Revenue Growth Planner

Let's go through each part of the planner.

### This Week's Dates

Write in today's date range.

### Your à la Carte Communications Menu

The list on the right includes all of the communications actions discussed in this book. They're listed here for easy reference. Simply select one and drop it into a day to the left.

NAME

Date Range:

## The 15-Minute Marketing® Planner

### This Week's Top Three Revenue Growth Priorities

1. _____
2. _____
3. _____

| 15-Minute Action | Outcome / Result<br>Success? Did you do it? |
|---|---|
| **MON**<br>Time: | |
| **TUE**<br>Time: | |
| **WED**<br>Time: | |
| **THU**<br>Time: | |
| **FRI**<br>Time: | |

**Growth Action List:**

*Choose from this list or create your own action!*

5-10 Min Customer Calls
Ask for a Testimonial
Communicate a Testimonial
Write a Case Study
Communicate a Case Study
"Did You Know" Question
Obtain Referrals
Follow Up on Quotes
Send Hand-Written Notes
Build Your Lists:
*All Past & Current Clients*
*All Past & Current Prospects*
Categorize Your Lists
Send Newsletter
Organize & Market Webinar
Book Speech(es)
Customers/Prospect Event
Write & Distrib. White Paper
Plan & Record Videos
Distribute Videos to Buyers
Obtain Press Coverage
WOW Action For Customers
Update a Page on Website
Send This Page to Buyer
Raise Prices

**Marketing Action Notes:**

_____
_____
_____
_____

**Who Will Hold
You Accountable?**

Check-In Date/Time:

**Bold Value Statement:**
Example: I help my customers attain their dreams.

**Figure 44.1    The 15-Minute Revenue Growth Planner**

## Your Top Three Revenue Growth Priorities

Now, write in this week's top revenue growth priorities. Think of this as open planning space. Use it for your major focuses for the coming week. Perhaps you want to gather testimonials. Or maybe you want to concentrate on following up on three major quotes. You might write in "throw together a starter list of customers and prospects." Maybe you want to practice behaving more boldly and confidently with customers this week. Anything is fair game here.

### 15-Minute Action

Now, Monday through Friday, look at the list to the right, and write in one activity a day. Monday might be asking for a testimonial, and Tuesday can be communicating it. Wednesday can be asking the "did you know" question, and Thursday can be following up on a quote. On Friday, you might send a handwritten note.

Conversely, you might want to ask the "did you know" question *every* day of the week, and that's perfectly reasonable.

If you read through the 22 techniques in this book, and the ones that resonated best with you are asking for referrals and communicating case studies, then just focus on those two.

Optionally, you can write in the time of day you are going to take this action. However, if you intend to do this work as a part of existing phone calls, then don't set a specific time, and you may actually take more than one communication action a day. No downside to that.

### Outcome/Result (Success? Did You Do It?)

This is the newest column in the Planner. It's here for you and your team to track your success. Did you get the testimonial? What happened when you asked the "did you know" question? Did you close the business when you followed up on the quote?

Keep track of your outcomes here.

It'll motivate you.

It'll move you to further action.

And it'll remind you that people are not offended or turned off when you communicate with them.

Rather, they are usually pleased and honored to have been chosen.

## *Marketing Action Notes*

This is a place for reminders, and other items. If you want to capture a conversation note in regards to one of your actions above, put it here. It has no specific purpose besides helping you remember specific details in preparation for your actions, or in their implemention.

## *Accountability*

If you are working this program companywide, then the people holding you accountable will be your managers, executives, and/or ownership.

Write in the specific names here.

If you're doing this solo, talk through your plan with somebody, and ask that individual to hold you accountable. I work alone, without staff, so my wife often serves this purpose. You need somebody to check in with, to ask you questions, and to share results with. Write in this person's name here.

## *Bold Value Statement*

This is the sentence or statement that helps you get this work done. It can be something like:

> "My customers deserve to do more business with me."
> Or: "I owe it to my family to do this work."
> Or: "My company is the best in the world at this work."
> Or, one of my favorites from a client recently: "My customers cannot read my mind!"

Whatever moves you to action, write it here. This can be the same or different every week.

But I want you to write it down every week, which means you think about it every week. And I want you to see it every day. If you start thinking you are too busy or you start thinking about failure or rejection, I want you to read this powerful statement, which is the absolute truth, and use it move yourself to action.

## One Action a Day

Be sure you're writing in one quick action every day, not three or five.

The goal is to execute one new communication action a day.

If the "did you know" question gets good results for you, and you decide to ask it on multiple phone calls a day, that would be overexecuting and underplanning, which is exactly what you're supposed to do. If, conversely, you write in five did you know questions for Monday, but only get to three, you'll likely be disappointed. But the fact is you did a significant amount of revenue growth work that day, and there's absolutely no failure in that, only success. Don't overplan and underexecute. Do the opposite. It's better for you!

## Be Specific

If you're asking for a testimonial, identify *who* you will ask.

Same for requesting a referral.

And for following up on a quote. *Which* quote?

Write it in.

The less thinking you have to do when it's time to take action, the more actions you'll execute.

## Timing and Tracking

These planners should be filled out by Monday morning. Wednesday is too late.

By the end of the week, review your results and outcomes. Add them to a running list of successes, including the date of action, the action itself, and the result or outcome. For example, track your testimonials received (paste them into the list or spreadsheet you keep), "did you know" questions and responses, quote follow-ups and resulting business, referrals received. The success log will help motivate you to plan and take new action. Plus, it's just fun to see all the good work you've done since you started this program.

## Chapter Summary

- Use this weekly planner to organize your daily action. Spend 10 minutes planning your week so that you know exactly what communication to execute when the day comes.
- Plan one activity a day only, and if you overachieve you can celebrate that instead of feeling like you failed because you only took three actions instead of the five you planned.
- Track your successes and use them for motivation.

# 45

# What Sets My Most Successful Clients Apart (Accountability)

I have clients that grow by 30–40% in their first year with me, and I have other clients that grow by 5–10%.

Nobody does this work of talking with customers, changing internal mindset, gathering testimonials, and communicating with customers and prospects daily and sees their business contract. Nobody shrinks. It simply doesn't happen with this project. Even if you took no action, but attained the critical mindset shift of focusing on your great value instead of your products and services, your business would grow. That's because you'd be bolder, more confident, and you'd take more action. You'd execute more. You'd tell more people about how they'd improve if they bought more from you.

So, a few years ago I realized I needed to figure what separates my clients who grow the most from those who grow the least.

Why did some companies grow by 40% in a year, and some by just 5 or 10%?

When I looked at everybody, it became crystal clear.

The most successful companies, the fastest growers, hold their people *accountable* the most.

The greatest differences between the two groups of companies are as follows:

The fast growers had owners and management who told their people that they expected them to take one communication action a day and followed up to ensure they actually did.

The slow growers did not have owners or managers who were comfortable asking people to do new work, even though it was only a few minutes a day.

The fast growers requested their people share their successes company-wide. When somebody gets a testimonial, or a new order from a successful quote follow-up, he shared it with the entire company. This creates a success loop in which everybody wants to be recognized. People aspire to be the ones sharing their wins and being thanked and complimented by their bosses.

The fast growers enlisted middle managers to hold their colleagues accountable.

The slow growers got diverted by fires and spent their days reacting to customer issues and problems.

The fast growers even implemented tools like scorecards to track who was doing what. They ranked their people based on communication activities and shared their standings weekly.

## Accountability Details

There are five critical accountability techniques an owner or executive needs to implement to execute this program effectively:

1. **Request that every manager, salesperson, and customer service person fill out the 15-Minute Marketing Planner each Monday morning.**
2. **Track the outcomes.** List your staff, and put a little checkmark next to the name of everyone who submitted their plan on Monday. If they do not, ask them where it is. "You promised you would have this, where is it?" That is the key question to holding your people accountable.
3. **Request results for the current week's communication action by the weekend.** Ask your people to write you a short email explaining how their actions have gone. It should be delivered to their account-ability group (direct supervisor and any executives running the project). What happened as a result of their actions? Did they get their testimonials or referrals? What happened when they asked for a referral? When they followed up on the quote, did they get the business?

4. **Summarize results and distribute success.** Communicate to your team that you are paying attention and that you know who's doing the work and who isn't. Your summary email should be addressed to everyone participating in this revenue growth program. Compliment the successful implementers, and share examples of their results. Also, identify by name all those who did not do what they promised. They are letting you, their colleagues, and themselves down. Make it clear this is not acceptable to you by identifying them.

5. **Flit and float and check in with people.** Have quick conversations with your staff about how things are going. Drop in. Ask how you can help. Give tips. Support. Motivate. Encourage. Help. Be positive.

---

### Chapter Summary

- Accountability separates the fastest growing companies from the slowest growing ones.
- Executives running this project inside their firms must be comfortable with holding their people accountable.
- Insist that planners and summaries arrive on Mondays and Fridays, respectively.
- Summarize their outcomes, and call out the successful people, as well as those you haven't yet heard from.
- Visit with your team one-on-one, offering your help and support.

# 46 | Grow Forth and Execute

Now you know.

You have what you need.

You know the value of gathering powerful, positive feedback from your customers.

You know that you cannot outsell or outmarket your mindset.

You know that the key to growing your business is to underplan and overexecute.

Procrastination and perfection kill revenue.

Therefore, we must take action when it's good enough, not when it's perfect.

We will communicate, and then assess what we enjoy and what's working.

If we don't like it, we'll stop it and replace it.

If it's not working, we'll also stop it.

Then we'll substitute in another action, because we know it doesn't matter what we do.

We understand that the only thing that matters is that every day, more people know what they can buy from us, and how they will be improved as a result.

That's all we're doing, after all.

In this communication, just as in our work, we're simply helping people.

We owe it to our customers to help them more. And to enjoy the money that comes in as a result.

We owe this work to our families, our colleagues, our prospects, and most of all, ourselves.

We will communicate our value consistently and systematically, and our business will not have a choice but to grow.

Ready?

Fire!!!!

Then aim and adjust.

And fire again.

Keep on firing.

Always. Keep firing.

# Appendix
# Workbook for
# Launching the
# Revenue Growth
# Habit

This appendix is designed to get you started with your Revenue Growth Habit.

Go through these questions and answer them to the best of your ability. Don't dwell too long on any one question. Movement and progress is the goal. Quick answers, then move on.

Write your answers here, if they fit, or on a separate sheet if you prefer.

First, list three of your very good customers, including their names, titles and companies, below.

_____

_____

_____

These are people you should ask to interview, to collect testimonials. Next to each, write down the day and time you will ask them for a "get your feedback on how we're doing for you" conversation. This can be a call you make expressly for this purpose or an add-on to an existing conversation.

_____

_____

_____

_____

_____

_____

_____

_____

For each customer you've listed, identify three people—prospects, ideally, or customers you want to expand your business with—to whom you can *communicate* one of your existing customer's testimonials. So, you want three different people listed next to each good customer you wrote down above.

_____

_____

_____

_____

_____

_____

_____

_____

Now, write down three different customers. What are they buying from you today? List those products or services next to their names. Be brief, summarize where appropriate.

_____

_____

_____

_____

_____

_____

_____

For each of these three, identify three good "did you know" questions, including the specific products or services you will bring up to them as options.

_____

_____

_____

_____

_____

_____

_____

_____

Next, write down three good customers you're actively engaged with now, who you can ask for a referral. Identify what you will ask for. Will it be for connections to *their* customers or vendors? Will you ask for a connection internally at another department? Or will you bring up specific companies you know they deal with to look for a connection there? Be specific, but write quickly. No getting stuck! Speed is the goal.

_____

_____

_____

_____

_____

_____

_____

_____

Write down three customers or prospects you would like to send a hand-written note to. Repeats from names already listed are okay.

_____

_____

_____

_____

_____

_____

_____

_____

Identify three specific customers who are not among your biggest customers but who have the potential and capacity to graduate into that group. List them here.

---

---

---

---

---

---

---

Next to their names, write down what you will communicate to them to develop their sales volume. It can be a testimonial, a "did you know" question, or anything else we've covered in the preceding chapters.

---

---

---

---

---

---

---

---

Which customer will you feature in your first case study? By when will you write up your first case study, following the format in Chapter 20?

---

---

---

---

---

---

---

---

# Index

Accountability, 33, 220, 223–225
Accounts, working with, 100
Action(s), 209–210. *See also* Procrastination
  by job title, 203
  and research, 156
  taking, 211
Active and passive testimonial communication,
    112–114
Activities per day, 13, 28–29
Add on existing conversation, 129
Angry customers, 90
Angry runners, 55
Annual revenue, 162
Appearances, 11–13
Art and science of marketing, 42–43
ASAP call for referrals, 137–138
Askers ("did you know" (DYK) question), 130
Aspiration, 113, 186
Associations list, 181
Attorney, 128
Audience of revenue Growth, 4
Audio recording, 110
Automation of communication, 87
Awareness increase and sales, 127
Awareness percentage, 126
  about, 127
  for attorney, 128
  business growth, 127–128
  for manufacturer, 128
  for printer, 128

Best-kept secret, 56
BlackBerry tablet, 55–56
Bold value statement, 220
Book creation of case studies to potential buyers,
  123

Bragging
  vs. communication, 61–63
  vs. helping, 62–63
Brand awareness, 43
Business
  expert truth speech to, 179–180
  gross, 46
Business graveyard, 56
Business growth
  about, 125–126
  awareness increase and sales, 127
  awareness percentage, 127–128
  "did you know" (DYK) question, 128–132
  million dollar question, 125–132
  questions, 126–127
  reactive work vs. proactive work, 28
  summary, 132
Business growth with videos
  about, 184–185
  good videos creation, 188
  growth technique, 185
  how to share values, 188
  rules for effective revenue growth videos,
    105–106
  summary, 189
  topics for videos, 186–188
Business-to-business space, 54
Busy condition, 27–29

Case studies
  book of, 123
  customer, 24
  to website, 200
Case studies to potential buyers
  book creation of, 123
  by email on your list, 122–123

Case studies to potential buyers (*continued*)
  by email one-on-one, 121–122
  growth technique, 121–124
  to people who can buy from you, 121–124
  by postal mail, 123
  summary, 124
Case study from customer interviews, 118–120
Categories, 161, 163
Category usage, 162–163
CEO and owner interview lessons, 97–102
Clients, private events for, 176
Closely held companies rate
  products and services vs. marketing, 51–52
  rating explanation, 52–53
Communicating
  about ourselves, 72
  meaning of, 38
  systematically, 37
Communication action, 81–82, 224
Communication activity per day, 13
Communication techniques, 212
Communications
  activity, 13
  vs. bragging, 61–63
  consistency and regularity, 44
  with customers, 61
  group, 38, 46
  and helping, 83–84
  parallel tracks of, 13
  regular, 44
  and relationships, 193–196
Company description, 94
Company-to-many
  communications track, 11–13
  revenue growth techniques, 82
  track, 163
Complaints, 75–77
Connect to another company, 134–135
Consistency, 13
Consultants, 35
Contracts, 115
Conversation
  testimonial communication in, 113–114
  testimonial(s) starting, 91
Customer case studies, 24
Customer complaints, 75, 77
Customer concern, 29
Customer development models, 150–152
Customer interview lessons, 105–106
  customer information omission, 103
  customer information provision, 102–103
  good customers, 102
  interview lessons, 102–104

revenue language testimonials, 105–106
  summary, 107
  testimonial reviewing, 105–106
  testimonials, 104–108
  value discussion, 103–104
Customer knowledge, testimonial(s), 95
Customer list, 65
Customer model developments, 149–151
Customer problems, revenue growth, 5
Customer service group, 141
Customer service professionals, 130
Customer testimonial, case study from customer
    interviews, 120
Customer testimony, 24, 83
Customer(s). *See also* Interview lessons
  aspirations, 153
  awareness, 126
  case studies, 186
  complaints, 76
  concerns, 29
  conversation setting, 90–91
  development models, 150–153
  feedback on, 13
  focuses on, 205
  helping, 212
  information omission, 102–103
  large, 152–153
  laser focus on, 24
  medium size, 151–152
  mid-size, 149
  pictures of, 174
  positive qualities spoken about by, 71–73
  proactive conversations, 75–78
  problems with, 187
  on product catalog, 125
  product value to, 187
  and prospects sharing, 112
  and prospects sharing videos, 188
  relationship cement, 77
  smaller, 153
  smallest, 150–152
  special event growth technique, 175–177
  steady drip, 76–77
  success of, 200
  unhappy, 76
  value to, 95

Dance choreographing, revenue Growth, 87–88
Demonstrations, 167
"Did you know" (DYK) question
  as add on existing conversation, 129
  askers, 130
  asking, 204, 219

business growth, 128–132
  as stand-alone call, 129
  strategies for systemizing, 130
Dieting, 34
Differences
  in knowing and doing, 32–37
  successful clients and accountability, 223–224
Discipline, 32
Distance between knowing and doing, 32–33
Done by work, 16
Double-axis chart, 50
Duration, 89–90

Email on your list, 122–123
Email one-on-one, 121–122
Email signatures, 115
Email vs. snail mail, 168
Emotional words testimonial(s), 93–94
Endorsements, 7, 110, 193, 200–201
Entry/lobby area, 115
Evangelist customers, 53–54
Evangelist marketing, 176
*The Evangelist Marketing Minute* (Goldfayn, Alex), 165
Executives, 130
Expert truth speech
  to business, 179–180
  growth technique, 179–181
  speech writing, 180–181
  summary, 181

Facebook, 6
Failure, risks of, 211–212
Family, 23
Fast, simple and free, 3–9
Fast growers, 224
Fear, 3, 68–69, 78, 196, 209
FedEx shipping, 123–124
Feedback on customers, 13
Fifteen minutes a day, 216
Fifteen minutes or less, 82–83, 215–216
Fifteen-minute Marketing Planner
  accountability, 220
  bold value statement, 220
  fifteen-minute action, 219
  fifteen-minute Marketing Growth Planner, 217
  a lá cart communications menu, 217
  marking action notes, 220
  one action per day, 221
  revenue growth priorities, 218–219
  specificity, 221
  success and outcomes, 219

summary, 222
  timing and tracking, 221
  week's dates, 217
Fly-by customers, 90
Focus, 25
Focus on quantity vs. quality, 82–83
Follow up, 113, 219
Follow up testimonial(s), 92–95
Follow-up process, 142
Founders, 52
Four parts of case study from customer interviews, 118
Frequently raised resistance (FRR), 65–69
Friendship, 23

Geography, 162
Good customers
  vs. angry ones, 90
  customer interview lessons, 102
Good list core, for social media creation, 157
Good list of components, social media creation, 156–157
Good videos creation, business growth with videos, 188
Grow forth and execute, 227–228
Growth by white papers, 171–172
Growth of lists. *See* Social media creation
Growth plan, appearances, 11–13
Growth potential, 149
Growth technique
  business growth with videos, 185
  customers' special event, 175–177
  expert truth speech, 179–181
  growth by white papers, 171–172
  handwritten note magic, 145–146
  high potential small customers (HPSCs), 149
  inside sales people and/or customer service people, 204
  by job title, 203
  marketing manager or company-to-money track quarterback, 201–205
  million dollar question, 125–132
  newsletter for list, 165
  obtaining referrals, 133–138
  outside sales person, 204
  owner calls power, 140
  owners and upper management, 203
  price increase as growth technique, 195–197
  public relationships, 191–194
  revenue growth categorization, 161
  sales and customer service managers, 204
  seven-figure follow-up process, 141–144
  short case stories creation, 117–120

Growth technique (*continued*)
  social media creation, 155
  trade shows into revenue, 173–174
  webinars and new business, 183–184
  website for revenue growth, 199–201

Habits, new, 215–216
Hand raising, 12, 44
Handwritten note magic, 204, 219
  about, 145–146
  standing out of, 146–148
  summary, 148
  tips for sending, 147–148
Helpful, 8
Helping people, 12, 21, 179, 184–185, 212, 220
Helping vs. bragging, 62–63
High potential small customers (HPSCs), 149–153
Home page, 201
How to share values, 188
Hypermeasurer, 41

Impact, 21, 72, 112, 114, 145, 201
Implementation, 82, 85, 87, 163, 174, 220
Implementing, 4, 8, 12, 33, 39, 45, 85, 110, 135, 139, 165, 211, 224
Imposing vs. striving, 65
Industry, 162
Industry associations, 180
Industry conventions, 177
Inflation rate, 137, 195
Influencers, 38
Inside sales, 141
Inside sales people and/or customer service people, 204
Interesting point, 53
Internal communication, 110–111
Internal connection, 135
Interview lessons
  CEO and owner, 97–102
  customer interview lessons, 102–104
Invoices, 115

Job title, 162, 203
Journalists, 193

Key questions, 92
Knowing and doing
  differences in, 32–37
  distance between, 32–33
  weight loss, 33–35

Lá cart communications menu, 217
Language focus, 84–85

Lawyers, 128
Length, 165–166
LinkedIn, 6
List(s). *See also* Revenue growth categorization; Social media creation
  additions, 157–158
  associations, 181
  category examples, 162
  components of good, 156
  customer, 65
  definition of, 38
  growing, 43–44
  maintenance, 155–156
  organizations, 181
  people core of, 158
  places for, 156
  topic, 183
Low-hanging fruit, 59, 153

Mailings, 123
Manufacturers, 128
Marinating in positivity, 77–78
Marketing
  art and science of, 42–43
  deficient level of, 49
  definition of, 37–39
  effects of, 21
  measure meaning, 41–44
  and new revenues, 52
  opens when sales closes, 21–23
  opportunity in, 57
  predisposed against, 52
  as priority, 52
  pulls, 39
  quality, 51
  vs. selling, 12–13, 39
  thinking shift, 23–25
  time for, 52
  useful measures of, 43–44
Marketing manager or company-to-money track quarterback, 204–205
Marketing materials, 116
Marking action notes, 15-minute Marketing Planner, 220
Mass mail, 38
Measure meaning, marketing, 41–44
Measuring, 41
Media
  coverage, 194
  help of, 193
  industry, 194
  local, 194
  members, 192

relationships with, 205
revenue growth plan, 193
Message, on hold, 115
Microphones, 188
Million dollar question, 125–132
Mindset
  beginning of, 7–8
  outmarket of, 21–23
  revenue growth shift, 24
  shift, 24, 199
Money requirements, revenue Growth
    techniques, 84

New revenues
  and marketing, 52
  on right products and services, 56–58
Newsletter
  consistently sending, 31
  email vs. snail mail, 168
  frequency, 171
  growth technique, 165
  length, 165–166
  newspaper frequency, 166–167
  one-on-one actions start, 88
  parts of, 168
  structure of, 167–168
  summary, 169
  testimonial in, 115
  total time investment, 168
  value fill of, 165
  value of, 166
  video embedded in, 189
Newspaper frequency, 166–167
Niche industry, 180
Noise, background, 188
No-pressure setup, 90
Note-taking testimonials, 92
Numerical rating, 45

Obtaining referrals, 133–138
One action per day, 221
One-on-one communications, 44, 82, 87, 130,
    172
One-on-one communications track, 11, 13
One-on-one strategy, 130
Opens when sales closes, 21–23
Organizations list, 181
Outcomes, 224
Outmarket, 7, 21–23
Outside sales person, 204
Overplanning, 221
Overthinking, 215
Owner calls power, 140

Owners, 52, 62
Owners and upper management, 203

Paper for writing, 145–148
Parallel tracks, 13
Partners, vs. vendors, 113
Partnership, 23, 100
Passive testimonial communication, 112, 114–115
People, value for, 37
People types
  core four, 157
  current customers, 157
  current prospect, 157
  past prospects, 157
Per day activity, 13
Perceptions, 22
Perfection, 8, 58, 211–213, 227
Permissions, 91–92, 95–96, 102
Personal communication, 6
Phone calls, 34, 46, 66, 110, 113, 129, 132,
    140–141, 143, 187, 203, 219, 221. *See also*
    Referral requesting by phone or personally
Photos, 118
Pitches, 191
Plan execution, 210
Planning, 222
Plant the seed and harvest the fruit, 135–138
Plant the seed only, 136
Playbook, 55–56
Positive correlation, 211
Positive qualities spoken about by customers,
    71–73
Positive thinking, 78
Positivity, 75, 77–78
Postal mail, 123
Price increase as growth technique, 195–197
Price raising, 195–197
Printers, 128
Private events, 175
Private jet travel, 175
Proactive conversations, 75–78
Proactive sales growth, 5–6
Proactive work, 28–29, 140
Proactive work vs. reactive work, 28
Procrastination, 8, 17, 32, 156, 211–213, 227
Product catalog, 125–126
Product demonstration and tips, 187
Products and services, 49
Products and services rating, 51
Products and services vs. marketing
  about, 49–54
  closely held companies rate, 51–52
  interesting point, 53

Products and services vs. marketing (*continued*)
  marketing quality, 51
  new revenues on right, 56–58
  products and services rating, 51
  quadrants, 53–56
  summary, 58–59
Promises, 137–138, 165
Promotion, 168
Proposals, 115–116
Public relations people, 191
Public relationships
  growth technique, 191–194
  revenue growth, leverage the media for,
    191–194

Quadrants, 53–56
Quantification, 93
Questions
  business growth, 126–127
  follow up, 106
  quantifying, 107
Quotes, 115–116

Rating explanation, 52–53
Reactive work, 28–29, 141
Reactive work vs. proactive work, 28
Readiness, 8
Reasons for work, 15–16
Recording, 91–92
Referral harvest, plant the seed and harvest the
    fruit, 136–137
Referral requesting by phone or personally
  connect to another company, 134–135
  referral techniques, 135–136
  referrals, 134
Referral techniques
  internal connection, 135
  plant the seed and harvest the fruit, 135–136
Referral term, 134
Referrals
  about, 133–134
  ASAP call for, 137–138
  ask for, 67
  asking for, 204
  finding through, 41
  referral requesting by phone or personally,
    134
  referral term, 134
  summary, 138
  ways to ask, 133
  what to do with, 137
Relationship building, 192
Relationship cement, customers, 77

Relationships
  and communications, 193–196
  with media, 205
  public, 191–194
Reminders, 220
Repeating, 33–34, 213
Repurposing content, 171
Resistance, points of, 65
Resistance in common, frequently raised
    resistance (FRR), 65–69
Resistance items, 67
Revenue, source of, 42
Revenue growth, 79
  audience of, 4
  customer problems, 5
  dance choreographing, 87–88
  fast, simple and free, 3–9
  goals, 209
  keys to, 73
  vs. practice work, 29
  priorities, 218–219
  proactive sales growth, 5–6
  proactive work, 28
  simplicity of, 44–46
  summary, 9
Revenue growth categorization
  about, 161
  category usage, 162–163
  growth technique, 161
  list category examples, 162
  summary, 163
Revenue growth habit, 3, 11, 58
  activities per day, 28
  parallel tracks, 13
  readiness, 8
Revenue growth, leverage the media
  about, 191–193
  media plan, 193
  for public relationships, 191–194
  summary, 194
Revenue growth priorities, 218–219
Revenue growth shift, 24
Revenue growth techniques. *See also* Testimonial
  communication actions, 81
  communications and helping, 83–84
  company to many, 82
  dance choreographing, 87–88
  focus on quantity vs. quality, 82–83
  implementation as helping, 85
  language focus, 84–85
  money requirements, 84
  one-on-one communications, 82
  techniques, 84

telecommunication simplicity, 84
  working choices, 85–86
Revenue language testimonials, 105–106
Revenue precursors, 44
Risks, of failure, 211
Rotate focus as a company, 131
Rule of thumb, 111
Rules for effective revenue growth videos,
  185–186

Sales and customer service managers, 204
Sales rep, 98
Salespeople, 130
Sample case study, 118–120
Search engines, 41
Segmentation, 161
Self-limiting beliefs, 68–69
Selling, vs. marketing, 12, 39
Selling pushes, 39
Selling vs. marketing, 12–13
Seven-figure follow-up process, 141–144
Short case stories creation, 117–120
Short list, 90
Similar value, 135
Simple Revenue Growth Process
Simplicity, 45
  of revenue growth, 44–46
Slicing and dicing, 161
Sliders, 200
Slow growers, 224
Smartphone, 188
Snowflakes to blizzards, focus on quantity vs.
  quality, 83
Social media, 6, 41
Social media creation. *See also* Newsletter for list
  good list core for, 157
  good list of components, 156–157
  growth technique, 155
  list additions, 157–158
  list keeper, 158
  list maintenance, 155–156
  starting, 158–159
  summary, 159
Solution, 118
Spam laws, 158
Speaking, date and time for, 113
Specificity, 15-minute Marketing Planner, 221
Speech writing, expert truth speech, 180–181
Speeches, 180
Stand-alone call, "did you know" (DYK)
  question as, 129
Standing out, of handwritten note magic,
  146–148

Starting, 33–34
  and repeating, 212–213
  social media creation, 158–159
Statement, 220
Steady drip, 76–77
Sticky notes, 131–132
Story telling, 187
Strategies for systemizing (DYK) question
  one-on-one strategy, 130
  rotate focus as a company, 131
  sticky notes, 131–132
  track who gets asked, 131
Structure of newsletter for list, 167–168
Success
  and outcomes, 219
  struggle for, 16
Success loop, 62
Successful clients and accountability
  accountability details, 224–225
  differences, 223–224
  summary, 225
Suppliers, 98

Teaching moments, 186–187
Telecommunication simplicity, 84
Telephone use, 89
Tesla vehicles, 54
Testimonial communication
  about, 109–110
  active, 111–112
  in conversation, 113–114
  growth technique. *See* Testimonial
    communication
  internal communication, 110–111
  passive, 112, 114
  rule of thumb, 111
  summary, 116
Testimonial guidelines, 111
Testimonial reviewing, 105–106
Testimonial(s), 62, 118, 168
  book of, 110
  collecting, 204
  company description, 94
  conversation starting, 91
  customer conversation setting, 90–91
  customer interview lessons, 104–108
  customer knowledge, 95
  duration, 89–90
  emotional words, 94
  emotionalize, 93–94
  follow up, 94–95
  follow up techniques, 92–93
  good customers vs. angry ones, 90

Testimonial(s) (*continued*)
  key questions, 92
  lead-in for, 65
  names with, 67
  note-taking, 92
  one-on-one, 116
  page, 200
  permission to record, 91–92
  permission to share, 95–96
  quantification, 93
  received and tracked, 221
  repository of, 111
  reviewing, 105
  summary, 96
  telephone use, 89
  unread, 109
  way of doing, 96
Thinking shift, 23–25
Time, 65
  spending, 57
Timing and tracking, 221
Tips for sending handwritten note magic,
    147–148
Today, 5
Tomorrow, 5
Tools, revenue growth, 155
Top line, 7
Topic list, 183
Topics for videos
  business growth with videos, 186–188
  customer case studies, 186
  product demonstration and tips, 187
  story telling, 187
  teaching moments, 186–187
Total sales, 162
Total time investment, 168
Track who gets asked, 131
Trade shows, 179
  handouts, 173
  talk about, 174
Trade shows into revenue, 173–174
True beliefs, 69
Trust, 23
Twitter, 6

Ukraine, 15–16
Underexecution, 221

Useful measures of marketing, 43–44
  communications, consistency and regularity,
      44
  hand raising, 44
  list growing, 43–44

Value, 118–119, 166
  for people, 37
Value discussion, 103–104
Vendors, 100
  vs. partners, 113
Video cameras, 188
Videos
  brief and casual, 189
  customers and prospects sharing, 188
  lengths of, 185
  testimonial, 186
  topics, 186
  on *YouTube*, 186
Voice message, 139
Volume, 149–151

Watermarks, 147
Way of doing, 96
Webinars, 45
Webinars and new business, 183–184
Website
  case studies to, 200
  testimonial in, 114
Website edit, 200
Website for revenue growth, 199–201
Weekly newsletter, 165
Weekly notes, 110
Week's dates, 217
Weight loss, knowing and doing,
    33–35
Weiss, Alan, 42
White papers, 171–172, 204
Work
  done by, 16
  for, 15
  vs. impact, 72
  reason(s) for, 15–17
Working choices, revenue growth techniques,
    85–86

Yesses, 98, 136